LEARN KERAS

*Master Neural Networks and Deep
Learning with Python*

Diego Rodrigues

LEARN KERAS
Master Neural Networks and Deep Learning with Python

2025 Edition
Author: Diego Rodrigues
studiod21portoalegre@gmail.com

Published by StudioD21.

Important Note

The codes and scripts presented in this book are primarily

intended to practically illustrate the concepts discussed throughout the chapters. They were developed to demonstrate didactic applications in controlled environments and may therefore require adaptations to function correctly in different contexts. It is the reader's responsibility to validate the specific configurations of their development environment before practical implementation.

More than offering ready-made solutions, this book aims to encourage a solid understanding of the foundational topics covered, promoting critical thinking and technical autonomy. The examples provided should be viewed as starting points for readers to develop their own solutions—original and tailored to the real demands of their careers or projects. True technical competence arises from the ability to internalize essential principles and apply them in a creative, strategic, and transformative way.

We therefore encourage each reader to go beyond mere replication of the examples, using this content as a foundation for building codes and scripts with their own identity, capable of generating meaningful impact on their professional journey. This is the spirit of applied knowledge: learning deeply in order to innovate with purpose.

We thank you for your trust and wish you a productive and inspiring study journey.

CONTENTS

GREETINGS

It is with great satisfaction that I welcome you to explore, in a solid and practical manner, the fundamental functionalities and advanced features of the Keras library, one of the contemporary pillars in the development of deep learning models. Your decision to master Keras represents a strategic step toward professional excellence, reflecting an authentic commitment to mastering the technologies that shape the present and future of Artificial Intelligence.

In this book, "LEARN Keras – Master Neural Networks and Deep Learning with Python," you will find a rigorously structured approach, aligned with the TECHWRITE 2.1 Protocol, which respects the classical fundamentals of understanding and valuing the well-established practices of software engineering and applied science. Each chapter has been carefully crafted to guide you from the basic concepts of neural networks to the most complex and specialized applications, always focusing on clear technique, conceptual precision, and immediate applicability.

By dedicating yourself to this content, you position yourself in a distinctive manner in a scenario where deep learning expertise has ceased to be a differentiator and has become an essential requirement for professionals in data science, machine learning engineering, automation, and predictive analytics. Keras, with its intuitive interface and structure based on best practices, not only allows for quick prototyping but also for implementing robust and scalable models for production environments.

This book is recommended both for those who are beginning their journey in the field of neural networks and for experienced professionals who wish to consolidate their knowledge with a technical, direct, and highly didactic approach. A progressive structure ensures that you understand the internal workings of layers, the learning mechanisms, the training and validation flows, and the best strategies for applying regularization, tuning, deployment, and integration with ecosystems such as TensorFlow, Pandas, and Scikit-Learn.

Throughout the 25 chapters, each enriched with tested examples, commented common errors, validated best practices in real projects, and consistent practical applications, you will develop solid technical skills to face the most demanding challenges in the field of deep learning.

In a technical world where trends come and go, Keras remains a stable, didactic, and effective tool — and this book honors that tradition. By the end of your reading, you will have mastery over the construction, training, validation, and deployment of sophisticated deep learning models, enabling you to act with expertise in critical, complex, and highly demanding contexts.

Welcome to this technical and transformative journey. Solid knowledge begins with structured steps — and you are exactly on the right path. Have an excellent reading and study experience.

ABOUT THE AUTHOR

www.linkedin.com/in/diegoexpertai

Best-Selling Author, Diego Rodrigues is an International Consultant and Writer specializing in Market Intelligence, Technology and Innovation. With 42 international certifications from institutions such as IBM, Google, Microsoft, AWS, Cisco, and Boston University, Ec-Council, Palo Alto and META.

Rodrigues is an expert in Artificial Intelligence, Machine Learning, Data Science, Big Data, Blockchain, Connectivity Technologies, Ethical Hacking and Threat Intelligence.

Since 2003, Rodrigues has developed more than 200 projects for important brands in Brazil, USA and Mexico. In 2024, he consolidates himself as one of the largest new generation authors of technical books in the world, with more than 180 titles published in six languages.

BOOK PRESENTATION

The advancement of neural networks and deep learning has consolidated Deep Learning as one of the most transformative areas of contemporary Artificial Intelligence. With the growing demand for intelligent, adaptive, and high-performance solutions, mastering an accessible and powerful tool like Keras has become essential for professionals who want to build robust models, interpret results accurately, and apply intelligent solutions in real-world environments.

This book, LEARN KERAS – Master Neural Networks and Deep Learning with Python, was developed to be your definitive technical guide, combining a highly didactic approach with the solutions found in advanced applications. You will progress from the fundamental concepts of neural networks to specialized techniques in NLP, Transfer Learning, MLOps, and model explainability, all within the practical and modern structure offered by Keras and its ecosystem in Python.

We begin our journey in Chapter 1, with a specific introduction to Keras, its history, philosophy of simplicity, and integration with frameworks like TensorFlow. We present its advantages compared to other deep learning libraries and how it stands out in the current landscape as one of the most widely used options in both industry and academia.

In Chapter 2, you will learn how to properly configure your development environment, install Keras via TensorFlow, organize your projects with a professional structure, and test your first neural model with clarity and confidence.

We advance in Chapter 3 with the conceptual foundation of neural networks: artificial neurons, dense layers, activation functions, and the historical foundations that support modern deep learning. This chapter provides an essential theoretical basis for understanding the next stages of model construction and tuning.

In Chapter 4, we present the Sequential model in Keras, its simplicity and applicability in real projects. We build dense networks, adjust basic hyperparameters, and evaluate performance in a structured way. Next, in Chapter 5, we deepen our understanding of optimization algorithms and loss functions, which are essential for adjusting and evaluating model behavior during training.

Chapter 6 marks the transition to convolutional neural networks (CNNs), explaining how to apply Conv2D, pooling, padding, and convolutional filters to visual data. Chapter 7 introduces recurrent neural networks (RNNs), ideal for sequential data and time series.

In Chapters 8 and 9, you will explore the powerful variations of RNNs: LSTM and GRU, in addition to mastering the use of Callbacks for refined control of the training process, model saving, and learning scheduling.

In Chapter 10, we address regularization with techniques such as Dropout, Batch Normalization, and L1/L2 penalties, which are fundamental for avoiding overfitting. Chapter 11 presents practical data preprocessing and augmentation techniques, while Chapter 12 introduces the Functional API and Model Subclassing, allowing for more flexible and sophisticated architectures.

In Chapter 13, you will dive into Transfer Learning, leveraging pre-trained networks such as VGG and ResNet to accelerate the development of high-performance models. Chapter 14 presents Autoencoders and dimensionality reduction, while Chapter 15 explores GANs (Generative Adversarial Networks), opening the door to innovative applications such as image generation and data synthesis.

Chapter 16 introduces the use of Keras in NLP (Natural Language Processing), covering embeddings, tokenization, and seq2seq networks. In Chapter 17, you will learn how to monitor and debug your models with TensorBoard and internal activation visualization techniques.

From Chapter 18 onward, the focus shifts to preparation for production environments: we show how to save and load models, how to scale projects with GPUs and TPUs in Chapter 19, and how to perform Hyperparameter Tuning with Keras Tuner in Chapter 20.

In Chapters 21 and 22, we address monitoring, observability, and modern MLOps practices, integrating model development into continuous integration and delivery pipelines. Chapter 23 covers model interpretation, explaining how to make your networks more transparent and auditable with tools like saliency maps and Grad-CAM.

Chapter 24 explores the integration of Keras with other essential libraries such as Pandas, Matplotlib, and Scikit-Learn, consolidating interoperability between frameworks. Finally, in Chapter 25, you will learn how to deploy your models securely and efficiently in APIs, cloud services, or serverless architectures, always with a focus on reliability and scalability.

Each chapter is built according to the TECHWRITE 2.1 Protocol, ensuring optimized structure, technical precision, and progressive learning. You will find tested practical examples, clear explanations, common errors and their solutions, as well as recommended best practices for each step.

By the end of this work, you will be technically prepared to apply Keras with confidence in professional, academic, or research projects, innovating in real and impactful scenarios.

Welcome to the applied and structured study of Deep Learning with Keras. This is the book that was missing to take your technical knowledge to a new level.

CHAPTER 1 – WHAT IS KERAS?

Keras is one of the most accessible and popular libraries for building deep learning models, created with the goal of making the development of neural networks more intuitive, productive, and standardized. Over the years, it has established itself as one of the highest-level interfaces for building and training neural networks, used by companies, universities, and research centers in projects ranging from academic prototypes to critical systems in production.

History of Keras

Keras was created by François Chollet, a Google engineer, as an open-source project launched for the scientific and developer communities. From the beginning, its goal was clear: to allow improved deep neural networks to be built quickly and with as little friction as possible. Keras was not intended to compete with low-level frameworks like TensorFlow, but rather to serve as a higher-level abstraction layer that allowed developers to focus on architecture rather than internal engineering.

At the time of its creation, deep learning frameworks were mostly verbose, required deep low-level computing knowledge, and had confusing interfaces. Keras emerged as a direct response to this complexity, introducing a minimalist approach, based on pure Python, with a clear, modular, and extensible API.

During its early years, Keras was compatible with different backends such as Theano, TensorFlow, and Microsoft CNTK, offering flexibility in model execution. Later, it became the official frontend for TensorFlow, which further solidified its presence in the machine learning ecosystem.

This shift was strategic. Native integration with TensorFlow brought performance gains, easier maintenance, and direct access to GPU and TPU resources, MLOps support, and tools like TensorBoard, without requiring developers to abandon Keras's simplicity.

Integration with Other Libraries

Keras is now a high-level interface fully embedded within TensorFlow. This means that when importing Keras, the developer is accessing an API through the tensorflow.keras module, which ensures full compatibility with the latest features of the TensorFlow platform, such as model distribution, multi-device training, and conversion to TensorFlow Lite and TensorFlow.js.

Although it was originally compatible with Theano and CNTK, these backends have become obsolete and are no longer maintained in current versions. The focus has shifted exclusively to TensorFlow, which brought standardization and greater integration with production tools.

Even so, Keras remains extremely flexible and interoperable. It easily connects with libraries such as:

- **NumPy:** for array and data manipulation.
- **Pandas:** for preparation and analysis of tabular data.
- **Matplotlib and Seaborn:** for visualization of input data, evaluation metrics, and results.
- **Scikit-learn:** for preprocessing tasks, cross-validation, pipelines, and model comparison.

In addition, it is possible to encapsulate Keras models within Scikit-learn pipelines or convert them to formats compatible with ONNX, enabling export and use in other environments.

Comparison with Other Tools

Comparing Keras with other deep learning libraries helps understand why it remains the preferred choice for many professionals and AI engineering teams.

Keras vs PyTorch

PyTorch is currently the main alternative to Keras. Developed by Facebook, PyTorch also emphasizes flexibility and ease of use. However, it uses a more imperative and dynamic approach, which means that the model is defined line by line and executed immediately. This gives PyTorch great control and debugging capabilities, making it especially valued in research and experimentation environments.

Keras, especially via TensorFlow, uses a more declarative approach, where the model structure is defined more statically and then compiled. This is advantageous for production environments, as it facilitates export, optimization, and deployment. With the advent of TensorFlow 2.x, Keras incorporated dynamic execution with tf.function, further approaching PyTorch's flexibility.

Keras vs Caffe

Caffe was one of the pioneering frameworks in convolutional networks, initially widely used in computer vision applications. However, its configuration-file-based structure instead of Python code became cumbersome and less intuitive for complex tasks. Today, it is considered obsolete for most projects.

Keras vs MXNet

MXNet was adopted by Amazon as the official backend for AWS Deep Learning AMI. While it has good scalability features, its community is smaller and documentation more limited compared to the Keras/TensorFlow ecosystem.

Keras vs JAX and other recent approaches

JAX is an emerging framework, highly valued in research projects by Google DeepMind. Its auto-differentiation and performance capabilities are impressive, but it still requires greater familiarity with functional programming and more abstract mathematical concepts, making it less accessible for most developers. Keras remains more user-friendly for learning, prototyping, and production transition.

Common Errors and Solutions

Adopting Keras is usually smooth, but there are recurring pitfalls, especially for beginners.

Error: Importing the wrong version of Keras

With the evolution of TensorFlow, many old tutorials use import keras, which refers to the standalone version, now discontinued. The correct way to import is:

python

```
from tensorflow import keras
```

This ensures compatibility with all modern functionalities.

Error: Compiling the model with incompatible parameters

Using incorrect loss functions or metrics for the model's output type causes runtime errors.

Example: Using categorical_crossentropy with scalar output instead of one-hot encoded.

Solution: Check the format of y_train. If you're using integer labels (e.g., 0, 1, 2), use sparse_categorical_crossentropy. If labels are in one-hot format, use categorical_crossentropy.

Error: Models not converging during training

Training neural networks requires balance between architecture, activation functions, optimizers, and data normalization. A common mistake is starting with a network that is too deep or poorly tuned, which may lead to unstable gradients or no learning at all.

Solution: Start with a simple architecture, normalize your data, and monitor metrics per epoch. Use callbacks like EarlyStopping to avoid overfitting.

Error: Forgetting activation in the final layer

When building classification models, it's common to forget the activation function in the output layer. This completely compromises prediction quality.

Solution: For binary classification, use sigmoid. For multiclass classification, use softmax.

Best Practices and Real Applications

Using Keras in professional environments follows a set of well-established best practices, which should be applied from the initial construction phase to the final deployment of models.

Build models progressively

Instead of trying to build a complex network from the start, begin with basic models. Validate that the data pipeline works correctly, that the data is well distributed, and that the model can learn the minimum necessary.

Use smart callbacks

Callbacks such as ModelCheckpoint, ReduceLROnPlateau, EarlyStopping, and TensorBoard should be part of the standard development flow. They allow you to monitor, adjust, and log model performance without the need for additional scripts.

Standardize preprocessing

Ensure that training, validation, and inference data go through the same normalization, tokenization, or resizing steps. An effective way is to encapsulate everything in a reusable pipeline.

Document the model architecture

Record the model structure, training parameters, and data

version used. This facilitates result traceability and makes the process replicable.

Use Keras for robust and productive applications

Companies such as Google, Netflix, Uber, and Airbus use Keras to prototype and scale deep learning solutions. It is applied in recommendation systems, fraud detection, predictive maintenance, medical image classification, legal text analysis, and much more. Its simple interface does not compromise solution robustness, as engineering principles are respected.

Keras represents one of the greatest achievements of applied computing in deep learning. Its ease of use does not imply limitations but reflects a carefully planned design, aimed at accelerating learning, facilitating development, and ensuring a smooth transition to production.

By understanding its history, differentiators, and native integration with the TensorFlow ecosystem, you will be ready to harness the full potential of the library in the coming chapters. This conceptual foundation will enable you to build models with confidence, avoid recurring errors, and apply well-established best practices in high-impact projects.

CHAPTER 2 – ENVIRONMENT INSTALLATION AND CONFIGURATION

All solid technical development begins with a well-configured environment. The use of deep learning tools such as Keras requires proper preparation, ensuring that the process of building, training, evaluating, and deploying models occurs without interruptions. A clean, versioned, and standardized environment prevents rework, facilitates collaboration, and makes the learning process more fluid. This chapter covers Python installation, Keras setup with TensorFlow, ideal project structuring, and best practices to maintain a stable and professional working environment.

Installing Python and Keras

The foundation of all development with Keras is Python. The recommended version is 3.10 or higher. Whenever possible, you should avoid installing libraries directly on the operating system. The use of virtual environments ensures dependency isolation, greater control over versions, and reproducibility across projects.

Python installation can be done via the official website or through Anaconda, which already includes useful tools such as Jupyter Notebook. However, the practical recommendation for professional and reproducible environments is to use venv (Python's native virtual environment) or virtualenv.

The sequence to create a functional virtual environment is as follows:

bash

```
python -m venv keras-env
```

This command creates a new directory named keras-env, containing all binaries and isolated libraries.

To activate the virtual environment:

On Windows:

bash

```
keras-env\Scripts\activate
```

On macOS and Linux:

bash

```
source keras-env/bin/activate
```

With the environment active, the next step is to install Keras. Since its incorporation into TensorFlow, installing Keras separately is no longer recommended. The official, reliable, and up-to-date way is to install TensorFlow, which includes Keras as part of its module:

bash

```
pip install tensorflow
```

This will install the latest version of TensorFlow, including the tensorflow.keras subpackage, along with other dependencies needed for CPU-based development.

For users with a compatible GPU (NVIDIA), it is possible to install the version with graphical acceleration, which significantly improves performance in long training sessions:

bash

```
pip install tensorflow[and-cuda]
```

Before proceeding, it is important to upgrade pip and other installation tools:

bash

```
pip install --upgrade pip setuptools wheel
```

The complete installation may take a few minutes. At the end, the environment will be ready for use with Keras within TensorFlow.

Verifying the Installation

Verifying the environment is an essential step to ensure that everything is installed correctly and that the packages are working. The following basic Python script helps check Keras functionality and the TensorFlow version:

python

```
import tensorflow as tf
```

```
print("TensorFlow version:", tf.__version__)
```

```
print("Is Keras available?", hasattr(tf, 'keras'))
```

If the script runs without errors and returns the TensorFlow version and Keras availability, the environment is properly configured.

You can also test the construction of a simple model with one dense layer:

python

```
from tensorflow.keras.models import Sequential
from tensorflow.keras.layers import Dense

model = Sequential()
model.add(Dense(units=10, activation='relu', input_shape=(5,)))
model.summary()
```

This code defines a sequential model with a single dense layer of 10 neurons, ReLU activation, and an input of 5 variables. The summary() command prints the network architecture and helps verify that Keras is operational.

Project Structure

Maintaining a clean and standardized project structure is essential for productivity, maintainability, and integration with automated pipelines. The ideal structure follows classical software engineering principles and modular code organization, according to the TECHWRITE 2.1 approach. The recommended model includes:

- data/: raw input files, CSVs, images, texts, or JSONs

- scripts/: modularized Python code with reusable functions and classes
- models/: trained network files (.h5 or .keras extensions), checkpoints, and training logs
- notebooks/: interactive notebooks for data exploration, prototyping, and technical documentation
- config/: auxiliary configuration files such as requirements.txt, .env files, and execution parameters
- outputs/: generated charts, geometries, exported files, and reports

You can create this structure using the commands:

bash

```
mkdir data scripts models notebooks config outputs
touch config/requirements.txt
```

The requirements.txt file is where the project's libraries are defined. A basic version includes:

text

```
tensorflow
pandas
numpy
matplotlib
scikit-learn
```

Using requirements.txt allows you to reproduce the environment on other machines with:

bash

pip install -r config/requirements.txt

This modular structure allows the project to grow clearly, facilitating testing, Git integration, and future deployment.

Common Errors and Solutions

During installation and configuration, some recurring errors may occur.

Error: ImportError: No module named 'tensorflow'

This error occurs when TensorFlow has not been installed correctly or the virtual environment was not activated. The solution is to review the activation steps and ensure that pip install tensorflow was executed within the active environment.

Error: Version incompatibility with the operating system

Some users face difficulties installing recent versions of TensorFlow on outdated operating systems or those without proper support for the chosen Python version. The recommendation is to keep Python up to date (ideally version 3.10 or higher) and use operating systems with active support.

Error: Use of standalone Keras version

Installing the keras package separately is no longer recommended and may cause conflicts. The correct way is always to use the tensorflow.keras module.

Error: Lack of GPU or incompatibility with CUDA

To use a GPU, the system must have a compatible NVIDIA card, updated driver, CUDA Toolkit, and cuDNN installed. In case of errors, the recommendation is to start with the CPU version to validate the scripts and then configure the GPU carefully, using the official TensorFlow documentation.

Best Practices and Real Applications

A well-structured environment accelerates development, reduces troubleshooting time, and supports teamwork. Among the most important best practices:

- Use separate virtual environments for each project to avoid dependency conflicts
- Version your requirements.txt and notebooks with Git
- Document installation commands and configuration steps in a README.md file
- Always start your notebooks with a library version verification block
- Use logs to record model versions and parameters used during training

In real-world projects, these practices enable experiment reproducibility, facilitate model audits, support team collaboration, and ensure reliable solution deployment. In tech companies and startups, organizing the development environment is often the difference between a successful project and an unstable product.

Correct environment configuration is the foundation for any Keras project. It ensures not only code execution but the stability of the entire development cycle. A standardized, tested, and versioned environment drastically reduces the risk of unexpected failures, accelerates development, and prepares the base for building robust deep learning models. By following the guidelines in this chapter, you will be ready to start exploring neural architectures with confidence and professionalism. The foundation is ready. Knowledge will now be built layer by layer.

CHAPTER 3 – FUNDAMENTAL CONCEPTS OF NEURAL NETWORKS

The development of modern artificial intelligence is deeply connected to the evolution of artificial neural networks. Understanding their foundations is essential to using Keras consciously, efficiently, and strategically. Building models should not be limited to replicating ready-made code but guided by solid knowledge of the principles that govern the behavior of each layer, each connection, and each activation function. This chapter presents the historical, conceptual, and computational bases that support neural networks and introduces a structural logic for the models that will be built throughout this manual.

Artificial Neurons: Biological Inspiration and Historical Evolution

The concept of a neural network arose from observing the functioning of the human brain. Biological synapses, responsible for communication between neurons, inspired mathematicians and engineers to simulate this behavior through computational systems. Initially, the goal was to replicate the biological structure precisely, which proved unfeasible. Over time, the focus shifted to an abstraction of functional behavior.

The first computational model of a neuron was proposed by Warren McCulloch and Walter Pitts. This simplified model performed a weighted sum of inputs and applied a binary activation function. Although rudimentary, it laid the foundations for future systems.

A major breakthrough came with the perceptron proposed by Frank Rosenblatt. It is a model with multiple inputs, adjustable weights, a threshold, and a binary output. The perceptron is considered the direct ancestor of modern neural networks. For a time, its limitations, such as the inability to solve non-linearly separable problems, dampened interest in the field. Years later, the emergence of the multilayer perceptron (MLP) and the backpropagation algorithm enabled significant advances. The combination of large data volumes, computational power, and new optimization techniques led to the field's resurgence.

Today, neural networks are used in areas such as speech recognition, computer vision, machine translation, bioinformatics, predictive modeling, recommendation systems, gaming, among countless other applications.

Layer Architectures: Perceptrons, Dense Layers, and Activation Functions

The architecture of a neural network is defined by how artificial neurons are organized. Each layer represents a transformation of the input data. The simplest layer is called a dense layer, or fully connected, in which each neuron receives input from all neurons in the previous layer.

A simple perceptron has a single output layer. However, for a network to learn more complex patterns, hidden layers must be added. This set of layers forms the multilayer perceptron, where each additional layer represents a new abstraction of information. The more layers and neurons, the greater the network's representational capacity.

Each neuron performs two fundamental operations: calculating the weighted combination of inputs and applying an activation function. The activation function is responsible for introducing non-linearity into the system, allowing the network to learn more complex relationships.

The most commonly used activation functions are:

- **ReLU (Rectified Linear Unit):** returns zero for negative values and keeps the positive ones. Widely used for its simplicity and computational efficiency.
- **Sigmoid:** outputs values between 0 and 1, ideal for probabilistic outputs in binary problems.
- **Tanh:** similar to sigmoid, but with output between -1 and 1.
- **Softmax:** transforms a vector of values into a probability distribution, used in multiclass classification.

The choice of activation function directly impacts model performance, especially regarding convergence during training.

Computational Foundations: Weighted Sum and Activation

The core of neural network operation is the weighted sum of inputs followed by the application of the activation function. Each input is multiplied by a specific weight. These weights represent the relative importance of each input. The sum of these multiplications is added to a term called bias, which adjusts the activation point of the function. This process is performed for each neuron in the network.

Error backpropagation allows weights to be adjusted to reduce the output error relative to the expected value. This iterative process is carried out during training using optimization algorithms such as gradient descent.

In Keras, constructing a dense network with ReLU activation and sigmoid output can be done as follows:

python

```
from tensorflow.keras.models import Sequential
from tensorflow.keras.layers import Dense

model = Sequential()
```

```
model.add(Dense(units=64, activation='relu',
input_shape=(20,)))
model.add(Dense(units=1, activation='sigmoid'))
```

This code creates a model with one hidden layer containing 64 neurons and an output layer with a single neuron. The input has 20 variables. The model can be used for a binary classification problem.

The Dense function represents the fully connected layer. The units parameter defines how many neurons the layer will have. The activation function is passed through the activation argument, and the input format is defined in input_shape.

Common Errors and Solutions

Error: The network does not learn even after many epochs

This may occur due to the choice of activation function, poorly designed architecture, or lack of input data normalization.

Solution: Use ReLU in hidden layers and normalize input data so they fall within a consistent range, such as between 0 and 1.

Error: Gradient explosion or vanishing

Occurs when activation values increase or decrease exponentially during training, preventing proper weight updates.

Solution: Use proper initializations such as he_normal for ReLU. Use robust activation functions and apply normalization within layers, such as batch normalization.

Error: Overfitting with very deep networks

Models with many layers may learn data noise, losing generalization capability.

Solution: Reduce the number of layers or units, apply dropout, augment the dataset with data augmentation techniques, and use cross-validation to measure performance.

Error: Incorrect activation function in the output layer

Using ReLU or tanh in the output layer can generate invalid results, especially in classification tasks.

Solution: For binary classification, use sigmoid; for multiclass classification, use softmax.

Best Practices and Real Applications

Building neural networks requires a balance between complexity and generalization capacity. The use of dense layers is ideal for structured data, such as tables with processed numeric and categorical columns.

When designing a model, start with a simple architecture and monitor its performance on validation data. Gradually increase complexity only if necessary. Always use activation functions and ensure that the data is properly prepared.

In real-world contexts, dense networks are used in time series forecasting, recommendation systems, customer classification, risk analysis, and predictive modeling in fields such as healthcare, finance, and logistics. The flexibility of dense networks allows their integration with other architectures, such as convolutional or recurrent, forming hybrid and highly expressive models.

Another recommended practice is using callbacks during training. EarlyStopping helps stop training when validation performance no longer improves, preventing overfitting.

ModelCheckpoint automatically saves the best-performing model, ensuring reproducibility.

Neural networks are not just sets of formulas. They represent the computational formalization of a powerful idea: the ability to learn from data. Understanding their foundations enables more efficient models, clearer interpretation of results, and more informed decision-making when tuning hyperparameters, choosing activation functions, and architecting solutions.

Mastering the concepts covered here is essential for the strategic use of Keras and for building models that go beyond experimentation and achieve robustness in real environments. The path to deep learning begins with these well-defined foundations. From here, the rest of the deep learning journey becomes clearer, more efficient, and consistent.

CHAPTER 4 – SEQUENTIAL MODELS IN KERAS

Building neural networks with clarity and precision begins with understanding the most straightforward structure offered by Keras: the sequential model. This is a linear and modular approach that allows stacking layers in a controlled way, enabling the construction of deep and dense architectures with just a few lines of code. With the sequential model, the developer gains immediate access to a progressive implementation flow, where each layer feeds directly into the next, following a unidirectional logic that simplifies debugging, tuning, and network expansion. This chapter details the construction, compilation, and training of sequential models, highlighting the use of dense layers, key parameters, and practices that ensure process consistency.

Sequential Structure: Concept of Sequential, Layers, and add() Method

Keras offers two main ways to build models: a sequential API and a functional API. The sequential API is the most direct and is recommended for models where each layer has a single input and a single output. This linear structure follows the traditional chain processing logic, making learning and implementation easier.

The Sequential() object represents the base of the model. It is initialized empty and filled with layers added in the order they will be processed. The add() method allows stacking layers that are applied sequentially, one on top of the other.

The basic syntax for creating a sequential model is:

python

```
from tensorflow.keras.models import Sequential
from tensorflow.keras.layers import Dense

model = Sequential()
model.add(Dense(units=64, activation='relu',
input_shape=(10,)))
model.add(Dense(units=32, activation='relu'))
model.add(Dense(units=1, activation='sigmoid'))
```

This code creates a model with three layers: a dense layer with 64 neurons and ReLU activation, a second with 32 neurons, and an output layer with sigmoid activation, suitable for binary classification. The input_shape parameter defines the input format, indicating that the model expects a vector with 10 variables. This parameter must be specified only in the first layer.

A sequential structure is recommended for supervised problems with tabular data or vectorized images, where there is no need for multiple inputs or internal branches. Its clarity facilitates understanding the architecture and tracking the data flow between layers.

Dense Layers: Building Fully Connected Dense Networks

Dense layers are the fundamental building blocks of sequential models. Each neuron in a dense layer receives input from all neurons in the previous layer, making it fully connected. This ensures that the network can capture complex relationships between input data and the target variable.

The main parameter of the Dense layer is units, which defines the number of neurons in the layer. The second key parameter is activation, which defines the activation function applied to the output of each neuron.

Dense layers are especially effective for problems where the data has already been preprocessed and is represented in vector form. They are versatile and allow the creation of networks with varying depths and complexities.

Below is a more robust version of a dense network for binary classification:

python

```
model = Sequential()
model.add(Dense(units=128, activation='relu',
input_shape=(20,)))
model.add(Dense(units=64, activation='relu'))
model.add(Dense(units=32, activation='relu'))
model.add(Dense(units=1, activation='sigmoid'))
```

This network has three hidden layers and one output layer. The ReLU activation is used in the intermediate layers for its computational efficiency and ability to mitigate the vanishing gradient problem. The sigmoid output transforms the final result into a value between 0 and 1, representing a probability for binary classification.

Compilation and Tuning: compile, fit, and Their Arguments

After defining the model architecture, it must be compiled before training begins. Compilation sets up three key elements: the loss function, the optimizer, and the evaluation metrics. These components will determine how the model is trained, how weights are updated, and how performance is assessed.

The compile() function performs this setup:

python

```
model.compile(optimizer='adam', loss='binary_crossentropy',
metrics=['accuracy'])
```

- optimizer: defines the weight update algorithm. The most used is Adam, which combines the advantages of SGD with learning rate adaptation.
- loss: the loss function used to measure the error between model prediction and actual values. For binary classification problems, use binary_crossentropy.
- metrics: defines which metrics will be monitored during training. accuracy is the standard metric for classification tasks.

With the model defined, the next step is training, done with the fit() method:

python

```
model.fit(x_train, y_train, epochs=20, batch_size=32,
validation_split=0.2)
```

- x_train: input dataset.
- y_train: corresponding labels.
- epochs: number of full passes through the dataset.
- batch_size: number of samples processed before weights are updated.
- validation_split: defines a fraction of the training data to be used for internal validation.

During training, Keras will display progress by epoch, showing performance metrics for both training and validation sets. This allows monitoring the model's behavior and detecting signs of overfitting or underfitting.

Common Errors and Solutions

Error: Missing input_shape parameter in the first layer

Without this parameter, Keras cannot infer the input size, resulting in a model build error.

Solution: always specify input_shape in the first dense layer.

Error: Mismatch between output activation function and loss function

If the model uses a softmax activation and the loss function is binary_crossentropy, the model behavior will be inconsistent.

Solution: for binary classification, use sigmoid with binary_crossentropy; for multiclass classification, use softmax with categorical_crossentropy.

Error: Learning rate too high or too low

If the learning rate is too high, the model oscillates without converging. If it's too low, the process is slow and may not reach global minima.

Solution: use adaptive optimizers like adam, which adjust learning rates automatically, or set manually between 0.001 and 0.0001.

Error: Stagnant accuracy metric

Accuracy may not improve for several reasons: limited architecture, imbalanced data, or preprocessing issues.

Solution: review the model structure, normalize the data, and apply balancing techniques such as oversampling or class weighting.

Best Practices and Real Applications

When building sequential models, using a progressive architecture is highly recommended. Start with a few layers and neurons, validate performance, and adjust as needed. Networks with too many layers and parameters can become unstable or suffer from overfitting.

Use callbacks to control training. EarlyStopping prevents unnecessary training after validation performance stagnates. ModelCheckpoint automatically saves the best model during the process.

Standardize data preprocessing before feeding it into the model. Scaling data between 0 and 1 or standardizing it with zero mean and unit variance improves training performance and stability.

Sequential networks are used in a wide range of applications, such as:

- Customer classification in CRM systems
- Failure prediction in predictive maintenance
- Medical diagnosis with structured data
- Credit and financial risk models
- Regressions for pricing and demand forecasting

The simplicity of the sequential model does not make it limited. On the contrary, it is a powerful tool for solving a wide range of problems, especially when combined with good engineering practices and systematic performance monitoring.

Sequential models in Keras represent the ideal entry point for applied deep learning. Their clear structure, combined with the ability to stack dense layers, allows for building highly expressive networks with minimal implementation effort.

By defining the architecture, build parameters, and training methods, the developer is able to deliver robust and efficient solutions aligned with best practices in machine learning engineering.

The journey with Keras is strengthened by this foundation. From this understanding, it becomes possible to explore more advanced architectures, customizations, and regularization techniques, always supported by the same logic: simplicity, modularity, and clarity. Each additional layer, each hyperparameter adjustment, and each metric evaluation becomes part of a conscious technical process, fully focused on results. This is the essence of sequential modeling with Keras.

CHAPTER 5 – OPTIMIZERS AND LOSS FUNCTIONS

Neural network models learn by adjusting their weights based on the difference between predicted values and actual values. This adjustment process is guided by two fundamental elements: the loss function, which measures the prediction error, and the optimizer, which decides how the weights should be updated to reduce this error. Understanding the logic and role of each is essential to building efficient models, interpreting their behavior during training, and ensuring solid and stable convergence. The proper use of these elements not only improves model performance but also reveals limitations and guides strategy adjustments based on the problem type.

Traditional Gradient Descent: valuing the past and manual iterations

The gradient descent algorithm is a historical foundation of neural network optimization. It is based on adjusting weights to minimize the loss function by following the direction of the negative gradient. At each iteration, the weights are updated slightly in the direction that most reduces the error.

This process requires calculating the derivative of the loss function with respect to the weights. The term "descent" comes from the algorithm's goal to descend the error surface in search of a minimum.

In practice, traditional gradient descent is rarely used alone, mainly because it performs calculations on the entire dataset at each step, making it slow and inefficient for large datasets. However, it serves as a reference for understanding modern optimizers.

A conceptual implementation would be:

python

```
weights = weights - learning_rate * gradient
```

The learning rate controls the step size taken in the gradient's direction. A value too high may prevent convergence; a value too low may make the process extremely slow.

The emergence of stochastic gradient descent (SGD), where weights are updated on each mini-batch instead of the whole dataset, brought significant speed and generalization improvements. Still, pure SGD may fluctuate, especially in loss functions with plateaus or unstable local minima.

Adam, RMSprop, and Other Approaches: differences, use cases, and convergence impact

To overcome the limitations of SGD, more sophisticated optimizers have been developed. Adam is currently the most widely used, combining momentum and adaptive learning rate techniques for each parameter. It calculates moving averages of the gradients and their squares, stabilizing learning even in deep networks or with noisy data.

When compiling a model in Keras, Adam can be called directly:

python

```
from tensorflow.keras.optimizers import Adam

model.compile(optimizer=Adam(learning_rate=0.001),
loss='binary_crossentropy', metrics=['accuracy'])
```

RMSprop is a variation that also adjusts the learning rate per parameter based on recent variance. It is particularly effective in problems with sequential data and recurrent networks.

Other optimizers include:

- **SGD with momentum:** accumulates previous gradients to maintain consistent direction and smooth oscillations.
- **Adagrad:** adapts learning rate per parameter based on update frequency.
- **Adadelta:** an evolution of Adagrad that limits the excessive accumulation of gradients.
- **Nadam:** combines Adam with Nesterov momentum, further improving stability.

The choice of optimizer depends on the nature of the problem and the expected model behavior. Adam is the default choice for most cases, while RMSprop may be preferred for time series problems, and SGD with momentum is useful when seeking greater manual control over the process.

Loss Functions: MSE, Cross-Entropy, and Common Variants

The loss function measures how much the model gets wrong. Its value is used to guide weight updates during training. The choice of loss function is directly tied to the model's output type and the nature of the problem.

The mean squared error (MSE) function is the most common in regression. It measures the square of the difference between actual and predicted values, focusing on minimizing absolute error while penalizing larger errors more heavily. In Keras, it can be used as follows:

python

```
model.compile(optimizer='adam', loss='mean_squared_error')
```

Binary cross-entropy is used for binary classification. It measures the distance between two probability distributions, treating the model's output as the probability of belonging to the positive class. It is applied when the output layer uses a sigmoid activation:

python

```
model.compile(optimizer='adam', loss='binary_crossentropy')
```

For multiclass problems, categorical cross-entropy is used. When labels are one-hot encoded, this is the correct function:

python

```
model.compile(optimizer='adam',
loss='categorical_crossentropy')
```

When labels are integer-encoded (not one-hot), the correct function is sparse categorical cross-entropy:

python

```
model.compile(optimizer='adam',
loss='sparse_categorical_crossentropy')
```

Choosing the wrong loss function can hinder training, even if the model architecture is correct.

Alternative loss functions such as Huber loss and log-cosh can be used in specific regression cases involving outliers or asymmetric data. In classification, focal loss can be used to handle imbalanced classes.

Common Errors and Solutions

Error: Loss function does not match model output

This often occurs when using an activation function in the output layer that is incompatible with the loss function. For example, using relu with binary_crossentropy.

Solution: use sigmoid for binary classification with binary_crossentropy; use softmax with categorical_crossentropy; for regression, use linear with mean_squared_error.

Error: Training stagnation

Stagnation occurs when the model stops improving the loss function. This may be due to incorrect learning rates, poorly prepared data, or overly simple architecture.

Solution: try different learning_rate values, normalize the data, increase network complexity, or introduce regularization and dropout.

Error: Overfitting despite low training loss

The model overfits the training data and loses generalization capability.

Solution: monitor validation loss, use EarlyStopping, apply regularization techniques, and augment the dataset with data augmentation.

Error: Unstable optimizer

Some optimizers are sensitive to weight initialization and data scaling.

Solution: use initializers like He or Glorot, normalize input data, and consider switching optimizers.

Best Practices and Real Applications

The choice of optimizer and loss function must always be based on the problem analysis. In regression tasks, avoid using classifiers for convenience. In classification, ensure that the data is well-labeled and properly organized.

Keep track of training logs and monitor loss evolution along with evaluation metrics. A lower loss does not always mean better practical performance, especially in classification with imbalanced data.

Use callbacks to reduce the loss function intelligently. ReduceLROnPlateau allows dynamic learning rate adjustment when loss stagnates, improving convergence. Combine with ModelCheckpoint to save the best-performing weights and ensure reproducibility.

In real applications, well-configured loss functions and optimizers make a difference in critical areas such as:

- Demand forecasting with high seasonality in retail
- Medical diagnosis with noisy and imbalanced data
- Fraud detection in payments with subtle and sparse signals
- Text classification with semantic ambiguity and multiple interpretations

In these scenarios, fine-tuning the loss function and optimizer significantly enhances model performance.

Optimizers and loss functions form the core of the learning

process in neural networks. Understanding their functions, specifications, and interdependence is a fundamental step in building reliable models. More than applying commands, mastering these elements requires technical reasoning, proportional judgment, and adaptability to different data types and objectives.

Carefully choosing the loss function ensures that the model is truly learning what it is supposed to solve. Using optimized optimizers ensures stability, speed, and consistency in the convergence process. Together, these two components form the engine of computational intelligence, which will be continuously refined throughout the development of solutions with Keras.

CHAPTER 6 – CONVOLUTION LAYERS (CNN)

Convolutional neural networks have transformed the field of computer vision. Their structure is based on well-defined mathematical principles inspired by how the human visual system processes images. The emergence of CNNs enabled tasks such as facial recognition, object detection, image classification, and segmentation to become automatic, accurate, and highly scalable. Unlike dense networks, which treat each input as an independent value, CNNs preserve spatial relationships within the data. This chapter presents the practical foundations of convolutional layers in Keras, including essential components such as Conv2D, pooling, and padding, culminating in the construction of a functional model for image classification tasks.

Overview: Roots in Classical Computer Vision

Before CNNs, feature extraction in images was done manually using filters and mathematical operators such as Sobel, Laplacian, and Canny. These techniques relied on prior knowledge of the visual structure of images, making systems dependent on specialists and poorly adaptable to new contexts. CNNs automated this process by enabling the network to learn filters directly from the data.

The first practical application of convolutional networks was in LeNet-5, developed by Yann LeCun, used for automatic reading of bank checks. This architecture already included convolutional layers interleaved with pooling and final dense layers, creating an efficient structure for visual pattern recognition.

With increased computational power and access to large labeled datasets, networks like AlexNet, VGG, Inception, and ResNet raised benchmark performance and were implemented in large-scale production systems.

CNNs are now the standard for tasks involving spatially structured data such as images, videos, 3D data, multivariate time series, and even biomedical signals.

Conv2D, Pooling, and Padding: Structural Components of CNNs

The core of a CNN is the convolutional layer, represented in Keras by Conv2D. This layer applies filters to the image, extracting local features such as edges, textures, and shapes. Each filter is a trainable weight matrix that slides over the image in small regions, performing multiplications and sums. The result is an activation map that highlights detected patterns.

The Conv2D function receives important parameters:

- filters: number of filters applied in the layer. Each filter will learn to detect a specific pattern.
- kernel_size: size of the filter matrix, typically 3x3 or 5x5.
- strides: how many pixels the filter moves while scanning the image.
- padding: defines whether the image size is preserved or reduced after convolution. 'same' preserves the size; 'valid' reduces it.

Example usage:

python

```
from tensorflow.keras.layers import Conv2D


Conv2D(filters=32, kernel_size=(3,3), activation='relu',
input_shape=(64, 64, 3))
```

This code creates a convolutional layer with 32 filters of size 3x3, applying ReLU activation to an input image of 64x64 pixels with 3 channels (RGB).

After convolutions, pooling layers are commonly used to reduce the dimensionality of activations while preserving the most important patterns. Pooling acts as subsampling, reducing the size of feature maps without losing the essence of visual information.

The most common layer is MaxPooling2D, which selects the maximum value in each region of the image. This reduces model complexity, decreases memory usage, and makes the network more robust to small variations in the image.

python

```
from tensorflow.keras.layers import MaxPooling2D
```

```
MaxPooling2D(pool_size=(2,2))
```

The combination of Conv2D layers followed by MaxPooling2D is standard in CNNs. After a few repetitions of this structure, the data is flattened with Flatten() and sent to final dense layers, which make the decision based on the extracted patterns.

Basic Architecture: Building a Simple CNN in Keras

A functional convolutional network in Keras can be built in a few lines, following a clear structure:

python

```
from tensorflow.keras.models import Sequential
```

```python
from tensorflow.keras.layers import Conv2D, MaxPooling2D,
Flatten, Dense


model = Sequential()
model.add(Conv2D(32, (3, 3), activation='relu',
input_shape=(64, 64, 3)))
model.add(MaxPooling2D(pool_size=(2, 2)))


model.add(Conv2D(64, (3, 3), activation='relu'))
model.add(MaxPooling2D(pool_size=(2, 2)))


model.add(Flatten())
model.add(Dense(128, activation='relu'))
model.add(Dense(1, activation='sigmoid'))
```

This model has two convolutional layers, each followed by pooling, and ends with one hidden dense layer and one output layer with sigmoid activation. It is suitable for binary classification of 64x64 pixel RGB images.

To train the model:

python

```python
model.compile(optimizer='adam', loss='binary_crossentropy',
metrics=['accuracy'])
model.fit(x_train, y_train, batch_size=32, epochs=10,
validation_split=0.2)
```

It is essential to ensure that the data is normalized between 0 and 1 and that labels are correctly binarized.

Common Errors and Solutions

Error: Incompatible input format

When building the model, an error may occur if the image format does not match the one defined in input_shape.

Solution: verify data format. Keras uses (height, width, channels) for channel-last format. Ensure that images were properly processed with libraries such as OpenCV, PIL, or ImageDataGenerator.

Error: Network output has more than one dimension

Convolutional layers maintain the 3D structure of the data. If Flatten is omitted, Keras cannot connect the output of convolutions to the dense layer.

Solution: always use Flatten() before adding dense layers.

Error: Overfitting with few images

CNNs are powerful but demand lots of data. When trained with few images, they may memorize the data and fail to generalize.

Solution: use data augmentation via ImageDataGenerator to generate artificial variations and improve model robustness.

Error: Excessive use of filters and deep layers

Too many convolutional layers and heavy filters in small datasets increase overfitting risk and make the model harder to train.

Solution: start with a few filters (32 or 64) and evaluate performance before expanding the architecture.

Best Practices and Real Applications

To avoid common issues in CNNs, follow these guidelines:

- Resize all images to a uniform size before training.
- Normalize pixel values to the [0, 1] range.
- Apply data augmentation with rotations, flipping, zoom, and translations.
- Use callbacks like EarlyStopping and ModelCheckpoint to prevent overtraining.
- Monitor accuracy and validation loss for signs of overfitting.

CNNs are widely used in:

- Medical imaging diagnostics (X-rays, MRI, CT scans)
- Facial recognition and biometrics
- Autonomous vehicles for real-time video analysis
- Industrial inspection using machine vision
- Security systems based on motion detection

Even non-image applications, such as multivariate time series analysis or audio signal classification, can benefit from CNNs by transforming the data into two-dimensional representations.

Convolutional layers represent a crucial technical advancement in the history of applied artificial intelligence. They replaced decades of manual feature engineering with an automatic pattern extraction process, making systems more accurate, adaptable, and capable of handling complex data.

Mastering Conv2D layers, efficient pooling usage, padding management, and the construction of compact and functional architectures are essential steps to applying deep learning with Keras in highly relevant visual tasks.

The simplicity with which these layers can be used in Keras does not reduce their conceptual depth or practical power. The more solid the understanding of CNN fundamentals, the more effective the application of these networks to real problems, yielding reliable and replicable results. The path is now open to explore more advanced architectures by combining different layer types, tuning hyperparameters, and applying regularization strategies. But everything begins with a well-structured foundation of convolutional layers.

CHAPTER 7 – RECURRENT NEURAL NETWORKS (RNN)

Modern artificial intelligence has evolved from models that process static data to architectures capable of handling dynamic sequences and temporal dependencies. Among the innovations that enabled this advancement, recurrent neural networks (RNNs) occupy a central position. Unlike dense or convolutional networks, RNNs are designed to process information in series, treating the order of the data as a fundamental part of the input structure. This ability to model temporal and sequential dependencies is particularly useful in tasks such as time series forecasting, natural language processing, machine translation, text generation, and signal analysis.

Understanding Recurrence: Links with Sequence Processing and Natural Language

The concept of recurrence is based on the reuse of the same set of neurons across multiple time steps. This allows the network to maintain an internal state that evolves with each new input, making it possible to store and use recent past information to make decisions in the present.

In natural language processing, for example, understanding a sentence requires knowledge of the previous words to interpret the following ones correctly. Recurrent networks can capture this type of dependency, even in sequences of variable length.

In practical terms, an RNN processes the input sequence element by element, maintaining a state vector that is updated at each new step. This update is based on the previous state value and the new incoming input. This process creates a chain of temporal dependence that, in theory, can span long portions of the sequence.

Keras facilitates the implementation of RNNs with its SimpleRNN layer, which represents the most basic form of this architecture, particularly as a starting point for understanding and prototyping sequential models.

SimpleRNN Layer: Traditional Structure, Stateless Flow, and Limitations

The SimpleRNN layer in Keras represents a direct implementation of the classic RNN. It accepts as input a three-dimensional sequence, where the axes represent respectively: samples, time steps, and features per step. Processing occurs over time, and each step influences the next through the internal state.

Building a network with SimpleRNN requires understanding the input format. Suppose a time sequence with 100 samples, each containing 10 time steps and 5 variables per step. In that case, the input_shape would be (10, 5).

Basic example of an RNN with Keras:

python

```
from tensorflow.keras.models import Sequential
from tensorflow.keras.layers import SimpleRNN, Dense


model = Sequential()
model.add(SimpleRNN(units=32, activation='tanh',
input_shape=(10, 5)))
model.add(Dense(1, activation='linear'))
```

This model processes sequences of 10 steps with 5 variables per step. The SimpleRNN layer has 32 internal units that process the temporal sequence, and the output layer generates a continuous value, indicated by the linear activation, suitable for regression.

The functioning of SimpleRNN involves three main steps:

- Reading one step of the sequence.
- Updating the internal state based on the current input and previous state.
- Repeating the process until the final step.

Despite its simplicity, SimpleRNN has important limitations. It tends to forget information from distant steps, a problem known as the vanishing gradient. This limits its application in longer sequences where older context is still relevant. To address this issue, more sophisticated architectures like LSTM and GRU were developed and will be covered later.

Sequential Forecasting Example: Implementing a Simple RNN for Temporal Data

A classic application of RNNs is time series forecasting. Consider a dataset with daily records of sales, temperature, or traffic volume. The goal is to predict the value of the next day based on previous days.

The first step is to prepare the data. Suppose we have a series of continuous values and want to use 7-day windows to predict the 8th day.

python

```
import numpy as np

def generate_sequences(data, window):
    X, y = [], []
    for i in range(len(data) - window):
```

```
    X.append(data[i:i+window])
    y.append(data[i+window])
  return np.array(X), np.array(y)


series = np.sin(np.linspace(0, 100, 500))  # simulated series
window = 7
X, y = generate_sequences(series, window)


X = X.reshape((X.shape[0], X.shape[1], 1))
```

The generate_sequences function transforms a univariate series into a training sample set, where each sample contains a sequence of 7 consecutive values and the target is the next value.

The model can be trained with:

python

```
model = Sequential()
model.add(SimpleRNN(50, activation='tanh', input_shape=(7,
1)))
model.add(Dense(1))
model.compile(optimizer='adam', loss='mse')
model.fit(X, y, epochs=20, batch_size=32, validation_split=0.2)
```

This code defines a forecasting model with a single RNN layer of 50 units, followed by an output layer for regression. The loss function is mean squared error, suitable for continuous problems.

During training, the model learns to capture temporal patterns in the sequence and uses the internal state to predict future values.

Common Errors and Solutions

Error: Incorrect input format

RNNs expect three-dimensional inputs. Feeding two-dimensional data causes an incompatibility error.

Solution: always use .reshape((samples, steps, features)) before feeding the model.

Error: Slow convergence or lack of learning

Simple RNNs may struggle to learn long or complex patterns. The network may show stable loss without improving performance.

Solution: increase the number of units in the RNN layer, normalize the data, reduce sequence length, or switch to an LSTM architecture.

Error: Overfitting with few sequences

If the dataset is small, the RNN may memorize the sequences rather than learning generalizable patterns.

Solution: apply cross-validation, regularize with dropout, or increase the data volume using shifted windows.

Error: Forecast error accumulates in multiple steps

When using the model to generate multiple sequential predictions, errors accumulate quickly.

Solution: reintroduce previous observations as inputs and apply correction using real data when possible.

Best Practices and Real Applications

When using RNNs, some practices improve model reliability:

- Normalize data to zero mean and unit standard deviation.
- Keep the number of time steps small for simple networks.
- Consider LSTM or GRU for tasks with long-term dependencies.
- Use dropout between layers to prevent overfitting.
- Test different activation functions beyond tanh, such as relu in deeper networks.

RNNs are widely used in:

- Demand forecasting in supply chains
- Sentiment analysis of short texts
- Human activity classification based on sensors
- Pattern detection in biomedical signals such as ECG
- Text generation and language modeling

The simplicity of SimpleRNN and its ability to model short sequences make it an excellent entry point to the field of temporal networks. In many industrial scenarios, recurrent networks are still a preferred architecture due to their efficiency in capturing ordered patterns.

Recurrent neural networks represent a qualitative leap in the ability of neural networks to handle sequences, time, and language. By maintaining an internal state that propagates through the input, RNNs enable models to understand contextual dependencies, making them advantageous in applications involving history, order, or time.

The SimpleRNN layer is an excellent entry point into this

domain, offering clarity in implementation and applicability in real scenarios with moderate complexity. Mastering its structure and behavior is essential for progressing to more sophisticated architectures like LSTM and GRU, which overcome the limitations of classical recurrence.

With the practices and fundamentals presented here, you will be prepared to build robust temporal models with Keras, applying deep learning strategically in sequential systems. The ability to understand time and order is a powerful differentiator in developing intelligent solutions. And the foundation of that understanding lies in well-applied recurrence.

CHAPTER 8 – LSTM AND GRU

Traditional recurrent neural networks, known as simple RNNs, were among the first architectures successfully applied to sequential data. They enabled the modeling of temporal dependencies in tasks such as time series forecasting, speech recognition, and language modeling. However, as projects became more complex and sequences grew longer, simple RNNs revealed serious limitations, especially in retaining long-term information. In this context, the LSTM (Long Short-Term Memory) and GRU (Gated Recurrent Unit) architectures emerged, offering concrete solutions to the most recurring bottlenecks of classic recurrent networks.

Motivation: How LSTM and GRU overcame the limitations of classic RNNs

Conventional RNNs update their internal states at each step of the sequence, propagating error gradients over time during training. While this mechanism works for short sequences, it suffers from two critical problems: vanishing gradients and exploding gradients. When gradients vanish, the network fails to learn relationships that are further back in the sequence. When they explode, the numerical values become unstable and the model fails to converge.

LSTMs were proposed to address these two structural issues. They introduce an explicit memory cell, responsible for retaining relevant information over longer periods. This cell is controlled by three gates: the input gate, which regulates how much new information will be added to memory; the forget gate, which decides what should be discarded; and the output gate, which determines which information will be passed on.

This refined control mechanism allows LSTMs to maintain a constant flow of relevant information without gradients vanishing over time.

GRUs, on the other hand, offer a simplified version of the LSTM concept. They use only two gates: the update gate and the reset gate. GRUs combine the memory cell and hidden state into a single structure, reducing the number of parameters and computational cost, while retaining the ability to learn long-term dependencies.

LSTM and GRU Layers in Keras

Keras offers native support for both layers: LSTM and GRU. Both can be used directly and are highly configurable for different application contexts.

The LSTM layer can be instantiated as follows:

python

```
from tensorflow.keras.models import Sequential
from tensorflow.keras.layers import LSTM, Dense

model = Sequential()
model.add(LSTM(64, input_shape=(timesteps, features)))
model.add(Dense(1))
```

The main arguments available in the LSTM layer include:

- units: number of units (neurons) in the cell
- activation: activation function for the output, default is tanh
- recurrent_activation: activation used in internal gates, usually sigmoid
- return_sequences: if set to True, returns the full sequence;

if False, returns only the last output
- dropout and recurrent_dropout: apply dropout to inputs and recurrent states, respectively
- stateful: allows the internal state of the network to persist across batches, useful for continuous forecasting

The GRU layer has the same essential arguments, with the advantage of being slightly faster in execution time, especially in tasks where computational cost is relevant. Its implementation is straightforward:

python

```
from tensorflow.keras.layers import GRU

model = Sequential()
model.add(GRU(64, input_shape=(timesteps, features)))
model.add(Dense(1))
```

The internal gates of LSTM and GRU act as selective filters. In LSTM, the input gate controls how much new information enters the cell; the forget gate controls what is deleted; and the output gate determines what is sent to the next layer. GRUs merge update and reset into a more compact mechanism, retaining control over what to keep and what to forget.

Applications in Time Series and NLP

The versatility of LSTM and GRU is evident in the two major areas where sequences are central: time series and natural language processing.

In time series, LSTMs are widely used to predict future values based on past sequences. A classic example is demand forecasting, where the goal is to anticipate sales volume, energy consumption, or financial asset prices. The ability to retain seasonal patterns or long-term trends makes these architectures superior to simple RNNs.

Below is a typical LSTM application for forecasting:

python

```
model = Sequential()
model.add(LSTM(100, activation='tanh',
input_shape=(X_train.shape[1], X_train.shape[2])))
model.add(Dense(1))
model.compile(optimizer='adam', loss='mse')
model.fit(X_train, y_train, epochs=20, batch_size=32)
```

In the NLP context, LSTM and GRU are fundamental for tasks such as sentiment analysis, machine translation, text generation, and seq2seq models. A sentiment classification model, for example, may use word embeddings feeding into an LSTM, whose final result is a binary prediction about the tone of the text.

python

```
from tensorflow.keras.layers import Embedding

model = Sequential()
model.add(Embedding(input_dim=5000, output_dim=128,
input_length=100))
model.add(LSTM(64, dropout=0.2, recurrent_dropout=0.2))
model.add(Dense(1, activation='sigmoid'))
```

```
model.compile(loss='binary_crossentropy', optimizer='adam',
metrics=['accuracy'])
```

For longer data or when parallelization is needed, GRU can be a more efficient alternative, maintaining competitive performance and reducing training time.

Common Errors and Solutions

Error: Incorrect input dimensionality
The input shape for recurrent networks must always be three-dimensional: (batch_size, timesteps, features). Using two-dimensional arrays will cause a shape error. The NumPy reshape function can be used to adjust the input correctly.

Error: Overfitting due to too many units
Using too many units in the LSTM layer without applying proper dropout or regularization can result in models that memorize the training set. Apply dropout, recurrent_dropout, and use cross-validation to avoid this issue.

Error:Incorrect use of return_sequences
Setting return_sequences=True when only the final output is expected causes inconsistencies. This argument should only be enabled if the output is a sequence corresponding to the input.

Error: Excessively slow training
In tasks with long sequences, using GRU instead of LSTM can significantly reduce training time without major performance loss.

Error: Loss of context between batches in stateful tasks
Using stateful=True requires extra care: batches must be correctly ordered, and the state must be manually reset using

model.reset_states() after each epoch or complete sequence.

Best Practices and Real Applications

- Normalize and standardize data whenever possible. Neural networks are sensitive to scale, and time series with large variations can impair learning.

- Standardize sequence length with pad_sequences, especially in NLP tasks, to ensure consistent input shape.

- Use callbacks like EarlyStopping and ModelCheckpoint to avoid overfitting and save the best weights based on validation performance.

- Monitor loss and metric curves with TensorBoard, identifying fluctuations and adjusting the number of epochs as needed.

- Start with GRU for initial experimentation, especially in problems with less data or limited hardware, and migrate to LSTM if necessary.

- Always evaluate the need for bidirectionality. Bidirectional layers are useful in NLP, where future context influences the current decision, but may be unnecessary or counterproductive in causal time series.

- Clearly separate training, validation, and testing, preserving the temporal order of data in time series and avoiding the use of future data to predict the past.

LSTM and GRU represent a milestone in the advancement of recurrent neural networks, solving historical limitations that hindered the effective training of models on long sequences. The introduction of control gates, memory cells, and selective retention strategies provided stability, flexibility, and performance for tasks once considered challenging. With Keras, applying these architectures becomes accessible, enabling the development of powerful solutions with few lines of code and maximum efficiency.

Technical knowledge of their structures, parameters, and internal behaviors, combined with practical application in time series and NLP, empowers professionals to explore new frontiers in artificial intelligence with confidence and precision. By deeply understanding how LSTM and GRU work, data scientists and machine learning engineers are equipped to handle complex flows, model highly variable sequences, and build impactful solutions.

The continuation of this training in the upcoming chapters consolidates this foundation, advancing to topics such as custom callbacks, regularization, functional architectures, transfer learning, and deployment strategies. The solidity built so far serves as the cornerstone for the creation of increasingly intelligent, adaptive, and robust systems.

CHAPTER 9 – CALLBACKS AND TRAINING CUSTOMIZATION

The training process of neural networks goes far beyond simply calling the fit method. Professionals seeking full control over the model's behavior across epochs use tools that enable monitoring, interruption, saving, and dynamic adjustments according to predefined metrics and conditions. These tools are known as callbacks. They represent an operational intelligence layer embedded in the learning cycle, ensuring greater efficiency, stability, and traceability during training. Proper use of callbacks allows automatic interruption when performance stagnates, saving the best models without manual intervention, scheduling dynamic changes in the learning rate, and even implementing customized logging and validation systems.

Callbacks: EarlyStopping, ModelCheckpoint, LearningRateScheduler

Keras provides a robust set of built-in callbacks. The three most commonly used in real-world projects are EarlyStopping, ModelCheckpoint, and LearningRateScheduler. Each of them has specific features that enhance automation and control throughout the training process.

EarlyStopping automatically interrupts training when a monitored metric fails to improve for a defined number of epochs. This prevents overfitting and saves computational time.

python

```
from tensorflow.keras.callbacks import EarlyStopping
```

```python
early_stop = EarlyStopping(
    monitor='val_loss',
    patience=5,
    restore_best_weights=True
)
```

This callback monitors the val_loss metric and halts training if it does not improve for 5 consecutive epochs. With restore_best_weights=True, the model weights are restored to the best validation performance.

ModelCheckpoint saves the model's weights during training. It can be configured to store only the best-performing model or all checkpoints.

python

```python
from tensorflow.keras.callbacks import ModelCheckpoint

checkpoint = ModelCheckpoint(
    filepath='best_model.h5',
    monitor='val_accuracy',
    save_best_only=True
)
```

The file best_model.h5 will contain the model with the highest validation accuracy, ready to be used in production without the need to retrain.

LearningRateScheduler enables dynamic learning rate adjustment across epochs. It is useful when starting with a high rate to accelerate convergence and decreasing it gradually for stabilization.

python

```
from tensorflow.keras.callbacks import LearningRateScheduler

def scheduler(epoch, current_lr):
    if epoch < 10:
        return current_lr
    else:
        return current_lr * 0.9

lr_callback = LearningRateScheduler(scheduler)
```

The scheduler function receives the current epoch and learning rate, returning a new learning rate. This allows implementation of classical strategies such as exponential decay, fixed schedules, or cyclical learning rates.

These three callbacks are often used together:

python

```
model.fit(
    x_train,
    y_train,
    validation_split=0.2,
```

```
epochs=50,
callbacks=[early_stop, checkpoint, lr_callback]
)
```

This block trains the model for up to 50 epochs but may stop early if validation loss plateaus. Meanwhile, the best-performing model is saved and the learning rate is adjusted progressively.

Creating Custom Callbacks: Traditional Approach to Logging and Hyperparameter Tuning

Although native callbacks are powerful, some situations require custom logic. Keras allows creation of personalized callbacks by subclassing keras.callbacks.Callback and overriding specific methods. This is useful for registering additional analytics, sending alerts, generating reports, or modifying hyperparameters based on business rules.

A basic custom callback structure looks like this:

python

```
from tensorflow.keras.callbacks import Callback

class MyCallback(Callback):
    def on_epoch_end(self, epoch, logs=None):
        print(f"Epoch {epoch + 1}, training loss: {logs['loss']}, validation accuracy: {logs['val_accuracy']}")
```

This callback prints the desired metrics at the end of each epoch. The logs dictionary contains all metrics computed at that point.

It is also possible to interact directly with the model:

python

```python
class LearningRateReducer(Callback):
    def on_epoch_end(self, epoch, logs=None):
        if logs.get("val_loss") > 0.4:
            new_lr = self.model.optimizer.lr * 0.5
            self.model.optimizer.lr.assign(new_lr)
            print(f"Learning rate reduced to: {new_lr.numpy()}")
```

This callback monitors validation loss and reduces the learning rate if it exceeds a certain threshold. This enables creation of adaptive and reactive training policies.

Another classical use case is structured logging in external files:

python

```python
import csv

class CSVLogger(Callback):
    def on_train_begin(self, logs=None):
        self.file = open('log.csv', 'w', newline='')
        self.logger = csv.writer(self.file)
        self.logger.writerow(['Epoch', 'Loss', 'Val_Loss'])

    def on_epoch_end(self, epoch, logs=None):
        self.logger.writerow([epoch + 1, logs['loss'],
logs['val_loss']])
```

```
def on_train_end(self, logs=None):
    self.file.close()
```

This callback creates a structured CSV log with key information from each epoch. This level of control is ideal for regulated environments such as financial, healthcare, or compliance-driven systems.

Real-Time Monitoring: How to Track Training with Greater Precision

Visual and analytical tracking of the model's progress is essential to understand how learning evolves, identify bottlenecks, and make decisions on early stopping or hyperparameter tuning. Keras offers native support for TensorBoard, one of the most established tools for metric visualization.

Using the TensorBoard callback enables logging of each epoch's training process:

python

```
from tensorflow.keras.callbacks import TensorBoard

tensorboard = TensorBoard(log_dir='logs')
```

After training, logs can be visualized with the command:

bash

```
tensorboard --logdir=logs
```

The dashboard displays graphs of loss, accuracy, learning rate, weight histograms, and other metrics over time. This helps identify patterns such as:

- **Overfitting:** decreasing training loss while validation loss increases
- **Underfitting:** high loss in both training and validation
- **Instability** from inappropriate learning rates
- **Premature** or delayed convergence

Besides TensorBoard, custom callbacks can be used to integrate with external systems such as dashboards, REST APIs for performance alerts, or integration with spreadsheets and databases.

Real-time monitoring allows long-running training to be supervised effectively, even in remote or distributed environments such as GPU clusters and cloud platforms.

Common Errors and Solutions

Error: Callback not triggered

If the callback is not listed in the fit method's callbacks parameter, it will not be activated.

Solution: Make sure the callback is included in the callbacks list during model training.

Error: Accessing unavailable metrics in logs

When using custom callbacks, accessing keys not present in the logs dictionary will raise an error.

Solution: Check available keys with logs.keys() or safely access them using logs.get('key').

Error: Saving models with inferior performance

Improperly configured ModelCheckpoint may save weights with worse performance.

Solution: Set save_best_only=True and select the appropriate monitor metric.

Error: Invalid LearningRateScheduler configuration

Returning incorrect or very low values from the scheduling function may cause training to fail or freeze.

Solution: Review the scheduler logic and keep learning rate values within a practical range.

Best Practices and Real-World Applications

In professional environments, callbacks are part of every robust training pipeline. Recommended practices include:

- Always begin with EarlyStopping to prevent unnecessary training
- Save models with ModelCheckpoint to secure and version the best weights
- Adjust learning rate dynamically with LearningRateScheduler or ReduceLROnPlateau
- Log all experiments with custom callbacks or experiment tracking tools
- Visualize metrics with TensorBoard or custom real-time dashboards

These practices are applied in companies and research labs that train large-scale models and cannot rely on manual monitoring. They improve reliability, save resources, and ensure reproducibility.

Applications such as medical image diagnostics, financial forecasting models, recommendation systems, and voice analysis all rely on callbacks to accurately control training progress and deploy only the best-performing models.

Strategic use of callbacks transforms model training into a controlled, automated, and transparent workflow. Rather than relying on fixed epochs or manual metric checks, callbacks offer a reliable mechanism to monitor, adapt, and record the model's performance across its evolution.

The ability to stop training automatically, save the best weights, adjust learning rate in real-time, and log custom metrics makes callbacks an essential component in any professional deep learning pipeline. Their proper implementation enhances technical quality and leads to robust, reproducible, and business-aligned results.

Mastering callbacks and their possibilities is a mark of technical maturity. With them, the learning cycle becomes intelligent, responsive, and ready to scale. This is the foundation of conscious customization in neural network training with Keras.

CHAPTER 10 – REGULARIZATION TECHNIQUES AND DROPOUT

As neural networks become deeper and more complex, the risks of overfitting increase. Overfitting occurs when a model learns the training data too well, capturing noise and specific patterns that do not generalize to new data. Regularization encompasses strategies aimed at reducing this problem, ensuring models are more robust, stable, and effective in real-world environments. This chapter introduces the main regularization techniques applied in neural networks with Keras, covering Dropout, Batch Normalization, L1 and L2 penalties, and demonstrates how these approaches complement each other to enhance the generalization capacity of models.

Overfitting: Reviewing Symptoms and Risks in Neural Network Projects

Overfitting is identified by the discrepancy between training and validation performance: while the training loss continues to decrease, the validation loss starts to increase. The main symptoms include:

- High training accuracy and low validation accuracy
- Validation loss increasing after a certain number of epochs
- Model learning too quickly but performing poorly on new data
- Inconsistent predictions when input contains small variations

Common causes are networks with too many parameters relative to the data volume, noisy or unrepresentative data, excessive training epochs, and lack of regularization.

Regularization is not a single technique but a set of complementary strategies that limit the network's complexity or control how it learns. The most effective techniques include Dropout, L1 and L2 penalties, and Batch Normalization.

Dropout: Implementing the Classic Idea of "Turning Off" Neurons

Dropout is a simple yet powerful regularization technique. During training, it randomly deactivates a fraction of neurons in a layer, preventing the network from becoming overly reliant on specific paths. This forces the network to learn more distributed and robust representations.

The central idea of Dropout is to simulate the training of multiple smaller networks, making the model more generalist. During inference (prediction phase), all neurons are used, and their activations are automatically rescaled to maintain consistency with training.

In Keras, implementation is straightforward:

python

```
from tensorflow.keras.layers import Dropout


model.add(Dense(128, activation='relu'))
model.add(Dropout(0.5))
```

In this example, half of the neurons in the previous layer will be randomly deactivated during each weight update in training. The value of 0.5 is common but can be adjusted between 0.1 and 0.6 depending on the network's depth and size.

Dropout is generally applied between dense layers. In CNNs, its use after convolutional layers can help, although techniques like Batch Normalization are more common in this context.

Batch Normalization, L1, L2: Theories and Practical Use in Keras

Batch Normalization is a technique aimed at stabilizing and accelerating neural network training. It normalizes the activations of each layer to have a mean close to zero and unit variance within each mini-batch, reducing gradient oscillation and allowing for higher learning rates.

In Keras, it can be applied as follows:

python

```
from tensorflow.keras.layers import BatchNormalization


model.add(Dense(64))
model.add(BatchNormalization())
model.add(Activation('relu'))
```

Normalization is applied before activation. This helps keep the network's data within predictable ranges, avoiding saturations and instabilities.

L1 and L2 penalties act directly on the model's loss function. They add terms that penalize large weights, encouraging the model to keep its parameters under control.

- L1 adds the sum of the absolute values of the weights (Lasso regularization).
- L2 adds the sum of the squares of the weights (Ridge regularization).

Keras allows these penalties to be applied directly to layers:

python

```
from tensorflow.keras.regularizers import l1, l2

model.add(Dense(64, activation='relu',
kernel_regularizer=l2(0.01)))
```

In this example, L2 regularization is applied with a penalty factor of 0.01. Very high values can hinder learning; lower values are generally more effective and safe.

L1 regularization tends to produce sparser models, where some weights are reduced to zero, useful in automatic feature selection. L2 regularization smooths weights, avoiding extreme values.

Regularization techniques can be combined in the same model. It's common to use Dropout, Batch Normalization, and L2 together to achieve a stable, efficient, and generalizable network.

Common Errors and Solutions

Error: Network with Dropout deactivated during training

Dropout only acts if the model is in training mode. In some custom workflows or when using model.predict during training, it may be deactivated.

Solution: Ensure model.fit is used correctly and that the model is in training=True mode if making manual calls.

Error: Loss does not converge with high penalties

Using very large values for L1 or L2 can dominate the loss function, preventing the model from learning the data's actual patterns.

Solution: Start with small values like 0.001 or 0.01 and adjust based on validation metrics.

Error: Unstable behavior with Batch Normalization

In some cases, incorrect ordering of layers (e.g., applying activation before normalization) can cause instabilities.

Solution: Apply BatchNormalization before the activation function, especially in dense networks.

Error: Improvement only in training, no impact on validation

If the model only improves on the training set despite regularization, it may indicate unbalanced or insufficient data.

Solution: Increase the dataset, apply data augmentation techniques, and review the training-validation split.

Best Practices and Real-World Applications

Applying regularization should be part of the standard design of any neural network. Established practices include:

- Using Dropout between dense layers with values between 0.3 and 0.5
- Applying Batch Normalization after convolutional or dense layers, before activation
- Including L2 penalty in all dense layers with many parameters
- Adjusting regularization hyperparameters based on validation loss and accuracy
- Monitoring the impact of regularization with callbacks and TensorBoard

In production environments, regularization prevents models

from learning spurious patterns, increases prediction reliability, and reduces the risk of failures when confronted with out-of-pattern data.

Real-world applications include:

- Anomaly detection in financial data with dense networks and Dropout
- Medical image classification with CNNs and Batch Normalization
- Time series forecasting in manufacturing with RNNs regularized by L2
- Models in edge computing with data limitations, requiring highly generalizable networks

These applications show that regularization is not a secondary adjustment but an architectural decision that determines the model's viability in real-world and production environments.

Regularization is the link between model complexity and its ability to generalize. Techniques like Dropout, Batch Normalization, and L1 and L2 penalties form an essential toolkit to ensure deep neural networks remain stable, efficient, and useful in real-world contexts.

More than just protecting against overfitting, regularization improves model interpretability, reduces reliance on manual adjustments, and allows greater confidence in results. In a scenario where data volume and variability continually grow, the ability to control learning defines the technical quality of a machine learning solution.

By mastering these techniques with Keras, developers position themselves at a new level of maturity, capable of delivering robust,

CHAPTER 11 – PREPROCESSING AND DATA AUGMENTATION

The performance of a deep learning model is directly related to the quality of its input. Effective preprocessing and data augmentation strategies are essential steps in building robust and generalizable models. Ignoring these processes results in networks with low predictive capacity, vulnerable to noise and struggling to adapt to real-world data. This chapter presents the most solid and replicable approaches for data preparation in neural networks, focusing on normalization, standardization, dimension adjustment, and artificial sample augmentation. The Keras preprocessing API will be explored with technical clarity and practical applicability, reinforcing its role in the complete modeling cycle.

Data preparation: normalization, standardization, and reshapes for images, audio, and text

Raw data is rarely ready to be used directly in neural networks. The preparation stage involves transforming this data to ensure it falls within appropriate ranges and has formats compatible with the network's layers. In images, audio, and text, these transformations must respect the temporal and spatial structure of the variables.

Normalization consists of transforming values to a standardized range, typically between 0 and 1. This facilitates training, avoids gradient explosions, and accelerates convergence. For images, the process usually involves dividing pixel values by 255:

python

```
x_train = x_train.astype('float32') / 255.0
x_test = x_test.astype('float32') / 255.0
```

Standardization refers to adjusting the data to have a mean of zero and a standard deviation of one. This technique is especially important in tabular data and time series, where the scale between variables can compromise learning. It can be applied using external libraries like sklearn before feeding the data to the model.

Reshape adjusts the data structure to the format expected by the network layers. For example, a grayscale image with 28x28 pixels should be converted to shape (28, 28,

When processed by convolutional layers:

python

```
x_train = x_train.reshape(-1, 28, 28, 1)
```

Audio data requires the extraction of spectrograms or MFCCs to transform one-dimensional signals into two-dimensional representations. In text processing, it is common to tokenize and convert words into sequences of integers or embedded vectors:

python

```
from tensorflow.keras.preprocessing.text import Tokenizer
from tensorflow.keras.preprocessing.sequence import pad_sequences
```

```
tokenizer = Tokenizer(num_words=10000)
tokenizer.fit_on_texts(texts)
sequences = tokenizer.texts_to_sequences(texts)
inputs = pad_sequences(sequences, maxlen=100)
```

This textual preparation converts sentences into fixed-length integer matrices, ready for input into Embedding layers or recurrent networks.

Data augmentation: generating new samples to avoid overfitting

When data is limited, the risk of overfitting increases. Data augmentation is the technique of generating artificial variations of original data to enrich the training set. This approach is very common in computer vision but can also be applied to audio and text.

For images, the most effective transformations include:

- rotations
- horizontal and vertical shifts
- zoom and cropping
- horizontal flipping
- brightness and contrast adjustments

These transformations do not alter the semantic meaning of the image but produce a network more robust to variations.

python

```
from tensorflow.keras.preprocessing.image import
ImageDataGenerator
```

```
generator = ImageDataGenerator(
    rotation_range=15,
    width_shift_range=0.1,
    height_shift_range=0.1,
    horizontal_flip=True,
    zoom_range=0.1
)
```

The generator can be integrated directly into the fit method:

python

```
model.fit(generator.flow(x_train, y_train, batch_size=32),
epochs=20)
```

For audio, techniques such as time-stretching, pitch shifting, and adding white noise can be applied. In the case of text, data augmentation requires more care to maintain linguistic coherence. Common strategies include synonym replacement, insertion or deletion of irrelevant terms, and slight syntactic reordering.

Libraries such as nlpaug and TextAttack provide tools to automatically apply these variations.

Data augmentation significantly improves model generalization, reduces the risk of memorizing artificial patterns in the training set, and is an indispensable technique in any project with a limited data volume.

Keras preprocessing APIs: ImageDataGenerator

and text analogs

Keras offers a consolidated API for data preprocessing and augmentation. The ImageDataGenerator is the most well-known, allowing real-time transformations during training.

In addition to geometric transformations, it allows automatic normalization based on the training set's mean and standard deviation:

python

```
generator = ImageDataGenerator(featurewise_center=True,
featurewise_std_normalization=True)
```

These options make the training pipeline more streamlined and flexible. Additionally, ImageDataGenerator allows loading images directly from directories organized by class:

python

```
flow = generator.flow_from_directory('images/',
target_size=(64, 64), class_mode='binary')
```

For tabular data or time series, Keras does not yet have robust native generators. In such cases, it is common to create custom generator classes using the Sequence pattern, which provides full control over data loading and transformation:

python

```
from tensorflow.keras.utils import Sequence

class MyGenerator(Sequence):
```

```python
    def __init__(self, data, labels, batch_size):
        self.data = data
        self.labels = labels
        self.batch_size = batch_size

    def __len__(self):
        return len(self.data) // self.batch_size

    def __getitem__(self, idx):
        x_batch = self.data[idx * self.batch_size:(idx + 1) * self.batch_size]
        y_batch = self.labels[idx * self.batch_size:(idx + 1) * self.batch_size]
        return x_batch, y_batch
```

This approach is useful in large datasets that do not fit in memory, or when preprocessing requires complex logic, such as physical calculations, specific transformations, or reading from external files.

For text, the Keras TextVectorization API offers built-in tokenization and standardization:

python

```python
from tensorflow.keras.layers import TextVectorization

vectorizer = TextVectorization(max_tokens=10000, output_sequence_length=100)
```

vectorizer.adapt(texts)

This layer can be inserted directly into the model, making preprocessing part of the architecture, which is advantageous in deployment environments.

Common errors and solutions

Error: training with non-normalized images
Images with pixel values between 0 and 255 cause network instabilities and may compromise training.
Solution: normalize to 0–1 by dividing by 255.0 or standardize using mean and standard deviation when appropriate.

Error: incompatible input shape
Convolutional models require data with three dimensions. Poorly formatted inputs will raise shape errors.
Solution: reshape data with .reshape(-1, height, width, channels) as needed.

Error: data augmentation applied during inference
Random transformations should be used only during training, not in prediction.
Solution: use only the original, preprocessed data during inference.

Error: inconsistent tokenization between training and testing
In text problems, using separate Tokenizers for training and testing leads to diverging representations.
Solution: fit the tokenizer only on the training data and reuse it on the test set.

Best practices and real-world applications

- Always normalize data before feeding it into the network, even if with a single line of code
- Use data augmentation whenever the dataset is small, especially for images and audio
- Check the data distribution after preprocessing to avoid distortions
- Use Keras APIs to keep code clean, organized, and compatible with the training pipeline
- Avoid applying extreme augmentations that may distort the semantic content of the data

In real-world scenarios, preprocessing and data augmentation are crucial for model stability and performance. Image diagnosis systems, legal text classification, financial time series forecasting, and sentiment analysis are examples of applications that demand special attention to data preparation.

Projects with heterogeneous or context-sensitive data, such as language analysis on social media or medical exam classification, benefit from well-defined and modular pipelines, allowing for fast testing and fine-tuning based on model feedback.

The success of a neural network begins before the first training epoch. The way data is prepared defines the boundaries of what the model will be able to learn. Preprocessing and data augmentation are not just auxiliary steps—they are fundamental to effective model engineering.

By mastering these techniques, the developer ensures consistency, resilience, and generalization capacity for the model. Integrating these practices into the Keras workflow expands automation, reproducibility, and performance in real environments.

A good network starts with good data. And good data only exists when it is handled with technical rigor and applied insight. This is the foundation for building intelligence that truly learns.

CHAPTER 12 – FUNCTIONAL MODELS AND SUBCLASSING API

Using the Sequential interface allows for prototyping simple neural networks in a direct and intuitive way. However, as the model architecture becomes more sophisticated, with multiple inputs, outputs, or internal branches, it becomes necessary to migrate to more flexible approaches. Keras offers two advanced alternatives for building networks with full architectural control: the Functional API and the Subclassing API. Both provide structural freedom, allowing the definition of dynamic flows, non-linear architectures, and integration between multiple data sources. This chapter addresses the main motivations for using these paradigms and how to apply them correctly in building production-ready models.

Limitation of Sequential: when the model requires multiple inputs, outputs, and branches

The Sequential API was designed for models in which layers are stacked linearly, one after another. This approach covers a wide range of simple dense and convolutional networks, but cannot handle structures that involve: multiple parallel inputs (e.g., combined image and tabular data) multiple outputs (e.g., simultaneous regression and classification) branched paths and intermediate merges architectures with skip connections (e.g., ResNet) networks with internal processing loops (e.g., complex autoencoders)

When these requirements are present, the sequential structure becomes an obstacle. Trying to force a complex model into the Sequential structure often results in redundant code, difficult maintenance, and limited extensibility.

In these cases, the functional approach allows for explicitly declaring the data flow between layers and building arbitrary architectures with clarity and precision. The subclassing approach offers even more flexibility, ideal for cases where the flow logic is conditional or iterative.

Functional API: defining complex architectures, merges, and branches

The Functional API is based on the explicit construction of a computation graph. Each layer is treated as a function that transforms tensors. By connecting layers as mathematical operations, it is possible to build models with multiple inputs, outputs, and custom internal paths.

The typical flow involves: Define the input tensors
Chain operations (layers)
Declare the model with inputs and outputs

An example of a network with two inputs and one output:

python

```
from tensorflow.keras.layers import Input, Dense, Concatenate
from tensorflow.keras.models import Model

input1 = Input(shape=(32,))
input2 = Input(shape=(16,))

x1 = Dense(64, activation='relu')(input1)
x2 = Dense(64, activation='relu')(input2)

combined = Concatenate()([x1, x2])
```

```python
output = Dense(1, activation='sigmoid')(combined)

model = Model(inputs=[input1, input2], outputs=output)
```

This model combines two inputs processed separately, merges the outputs with a concatenation, and returns a single prediction. This pattern is common in tasks that combine images and metadata, time series and categorical data, or multiple input sources.

The Functional API also allows for creating branches and intermediate merges. A classic example is the Y-shaped architecture, where a single input splits into two independent paths that are later merged:

python

```python
input = Input(shape=(64,))

x = Dense(128, activation='relu')(input)
branch1 = Dense(64, activation='relu')(x)
branch2 = Dense(64, activation='relu')(x)

merged = Concatenate()([branch1, branch2])
output = Dense(1, activation='linear')(merged)

model = Model(inputs=input, outputs=output)
```

This structure is useful when different neuron subsets learn distinct aspects of the same data, such as style and content in images, or semantics and syntax in text.

The flexibility of the Functional API lies in its ability to explicitly define the data path, controlling where flows split and merge, without limitations imposed by fixed sequences.

Subclassing: building custom models by inheriting from tf.keras.Model

For cases where the model logic cannot be represented using a purely declarative flow—such as conditional loops, dynamic structures, or reusable modules—Keras provides the Subclassing API. This model follows the object-oriented pattern, allowing the definition of a custom class that inherits from tf.keras.Model.

The Subclassing API requires defining the __init__ method to declare the layers and the call method to implement the data flow.

Example of a model with custom logic:

python

```python
import tensorflow as tf

class MyModel(tf.keras.Model):
    def __init__(self):
        super(MyModel, self).__init__()
        self.dense1 = tf.keras.layers.Dense(64, activation='relu')
        self.dense2 = tf.keras.layers.Dense(64, activation='relu')
        self.output_layer = tf.keras.layers.Dense(1)

    def call(self, inputs):
```

```
        x = self.dense1(inputs)
        x = self.dense2(x)
        return self.output_layer(x)


model = MyModel()
model.compile(optimizer='adam', loss='mse')
```

This structure is ideal for creating modular models, custom recurrent networks, conditional architectures, and solutions where the data flow depends on internal decisions based on the processed values.

Subclassing is also recommended for researchers and developers of new architectures, where model behavior goes beyond what static computation graphs can represent.

Common errors and solutions

Error: multiple outputs with a single loss
When using multiple outputs, it is common to forget to define a loss for each one or a weighted combination.
Solution: define the losses as a dictionary or list and adjust the relative weights according to the importance of each output.

Error: incorrect use of call in subclassing
The call method must return the network output, but omissions or incorrect returns cause silent errors or execution failures.
Solution: always explicitly return the processed output tensor.

Error: layers not tracked in the custom model
Layers declared outside __init__ are not recognized by Keras's

tracking system.

Solution: declare all layers as instance attributes within the __init__ method.

Error: inputs not used in functional models

Declaring an input tensor without correctly connecting it results in a disconnected graph error.

Solution: connect all inputs and outputs within the chain of operations using the Functional API.

Best practices and real-world applications

- Use Sequential only when the model is linear and straightforward.
- Adopt the Functional API for models with multiple paths, inputs, or outputs.
- Apply Subclassing when the logic involves conditions, loops, or dynamic structures.
- Maintain a clear separation between architecture definition (__init__) and execution (call).
- Document input and output flows in functional models to facilitate maintenance.
- Use model.summary() frequently to check if the computation graph is correctly built.
- Apply the Functional API in architectures such as ResNet, Inception, Siamese Networks, and complex Autoencoders.

Real-world environments with multiple input sources, sensor integration, multimodal data, and decision pipelines benefit from the flexibility of these advanced APIs. In recommendation systems, for example, inputs may include browsing history, demographic data, and product embeddings. In medical diagnostics, images are combined with laboratory tests, patient history, and clinical notes.

These scenarios require full control over how information is processed and combined, and the adoption of the Functional API or Subclassing becomes essential.

Mastering Keras's advanced APIs marks a technical milestone in the evolution of a machine learning professional. The ability to build customized, branched, and modular architectures allows for the creation of solutions precisely tailored to data requirements and project objectives.

More than a tool, the Functional API and Subclassing offer a new modeling paradigm. By abandoning sequential thinking, the developer learns to think in terms of data flow, decision paths, and integration of multiple sources. This opens space for architectural innovations and increases the sophistication of the solutions built.

Technical maturity lies not only in the depth of the models, but in the ability to structure solutions that mirror the complexity of the real world with clarity, control, and scalability. These are the tools that enable that journey.

CHAPTER 13 – TRANSFER LEARNING

The performance of a deep learning model is directly related to the quality of the input. Effective preprocessing and data augmentation strategies are essential steps in building robust and generalizable models. Ignoring these processes results in networks with low predictive capacity, vulnerable to noise, and with difficulty adapting to real data. This chapter explores the most solid and replicable approaches to data preparation in neural networks, focusing on normalization, standardization, dimensional adjustments, and artificial sample augmentation. The Keras preprocessing API will be presented with technical clarity and practical applicability, reinforcing its role in the complete modeling cycle.

Classic concept of reuse: valuing the initial research in deep networks

Transfer learning is rooted in the idea that knowledge acquired in one task can be useful for another similar task. Just as an engineer who understands electrical fundamentals can learn electronics more easily, neural networks that have already captured complex patterns in large datasets can be adapted to solve new problems efficiently.

The starting point for the massive use of transfer learning was the success of the AlexNet model, followed by architectures like VGG, ResNet, Inception, and MobileNet. These networks were trained with millions of images in ImageNet, one of the largest labeled repositories in the world, containing more than a thousand object categories.

By leveraging these networks, transfer learning eliminates the need to train all layers from scratch. Instead, the pre-trained convolutional base is used as a feature extractor, attaching a new classification or regression head for the final task.

This approach is highly effective in scenarios such as:

- medical image classification with few examples
- object identification in embedded systems
- defect classification in industrial products
- pattern recognition in satellite or microscopic images

Pre-trained models: VGG, ResNet, Inception, MobileNet and their practical applications

Keras provides direct access to several pre-trained architectures with weights fine-tuned on ImageNet. The model choice depends on factors such as depth, inference speed, model size, and the type of deployment device.

The main options are:

- VGG16 and VGG19: deep networks with simple convolutional blocks. Easy to understand and modify but memory-intensive.
- ResNet50: introduces residual blocks with shortcut connections, enabling very deep and stable networks.
- InceptionV3: uses multiple filter sizes in parallel, learning patterns at different scales.
- MobileNet: designed for mobile devices, with a lightweight and fast architecture, ideal for edge computing.

Loading a pre-trained model is done with a single call:

python

from tensorflow.keras.applications import VGG16

```
base_model = VGG16(weights='imagenet', include_top=False,
input_shape=(224, 224, 3))
```

By setting include_top=False, the final classification layer is removed, keeping only the convolutional layers as feature extractors. The new head is added with customized dense layers:

python

```
from tensorflow.keras.models import Model
from tensorflow.keras.layers import Flatten, Dense

x = base_model.output
x = Flatten()(x)
x = Dense(128, activation='relu')(x)
output = Dense(1, activation='sigmoid')(x)

model = Model(inputs=base_model.input, outputs=output)
```

This approach connects the base output to a simple binary classifier, which can be trained with the task-specific data.

Freezing layers and fine tuning: how to adjust weights and manage different learning stages

The main strategy when using transfer learning involves two stages: freezing and fine tuning.

In the first stage, all layers of the base model are frozen, meaning their weights will not be updated during training. This ensures that the knowledge learned from the original dataset (such as edges, shapes, and textures) is preserved.

python

```
for layer in base_model.layers:
    layer.trainable = False
```

Then, the model is compiled and trained with the new task data:

python

```
model.compile(optimizer='adam', loss='binary_crossentropy', metrics=['accuracy'])
model.fit(x_train, y_train, epochs=10, validation_split=0.2)
```

This training adjusts only the newly added layers, allowing the model to adapt without compromising the convolutional base.

After this first stage, fine tuning can be performed. Fine tuning consists of partially unfreezing the last convolutional layers and continuing the training with a lower learning rate. This allows the network to refine its filters based on the specifics of the new task.

python

```
for layer in base_model.layers[-4:]:
    layer.trainable = True
```

```
model.compile(optimizer=tf.keras.optimizers.Adam(learning_rate=1e-5), loss='binary_crossentropy', metrics=['accuracy'])
model.fit(x_train, y_train, epochs=5, validation_split=0.2)
```

The lower learning rate prevents the weights trained on ImageNet from being quickly overwritten, promoting gradual refinement.

The number of layers to unfreeze depends on the similarity between tasks. If the new data is very different from the original, more layers can be adjusted. If the tasks are similar, it's better to keep most layers frozen.

Common errors and solutions

Error: model doesn't learn after loading the base
Training the new head without unfreezing any layers may lead to a model that doesn't adapt well.
Solution: after training the top layers, perform fine tuning by unfreezing the last convolutional layers.

Error: increasing loss during fine tuning
Training the entire model with a high learning rate degrades the pre-trained weights.
Solution: use a lower learning rate during fine tuning and monitor validation metrics.

Error: incorrect input dimensions
Each pre-trained model requires a specific minimum input size. VGG16 and ResNet50, for example, require $(224, 224, 3)$.
Solution: resize the images with cv2.resize or ImageDataGenerator with target_size=(224,224).

Error: forgetting to recompile after changing trainable
After unfreezing layers, the model must be recompiled so that Keras updates the trainable parameters.

Solution: call compile again before continuing training.

Best practices and real-world applications

- use include_top=False when loading pre-trained models to add custom layers
- always start with the base layers frozen and train only the final layers
- use data augmentation during training with frozen base to avoid overfitting
- apply fine tuning with a small learning rate and few epochs
- choose the base model considering the balance between performance and inference time
- save checkpoints during training to restore the best model

Transfer learning is widely used in areas such as:

- diagnostic imaging (tumor detection, x-ray analysis)
- security (facial recognition, surveillance analysis)
- agriculture (leaf disease classification, fruit counting)
- mobility (license plate reading, obstacle detection)
- retail (product classification, shelf analysis)

Companies and institutions use this approach to leverage the intelligence of global models and apply it to specific contexts, with low computational cost and high effectiveness.

Transfer learning represents a turning point in the democratization of deep learning. By reusing the knowledge of large-scale trained models, artificial intelligence can be applied in contexts with limited data, restricted resources, and the need for high precision.

More than a technique, it is a philosophy of conscious reuse, valuing the computational effort invested by major labs and bringing its benefits to local, focused, and specialized applications.

Mastering this approach transforms the way deep learning solutions are built, allowing any project, regardless of its scale, to access the state of the art in computer vision. It's a resource that enables quality leaps with savings in time, energy, and investment. And that is what makes transfer learning a strategic tool for any applied AI professional.

CHAPTER 14 – AUTOENCODERS AND DIMENSIONALITY REDUCTION

Traditional neural networks are designed to predict an output from an input. Autoencoders invert this logic, learning to reconstruct the input itself as output. Although this behavior may seem redundant, it allows the network to learn compressed, efficient, and informative representations of the data, capturing their essence in a lower-dimensional space. This ability makes them powerful tools for dimensionality reduction, data compression, anomaly detection, and unsupervised preprocessing. In this chapter, we will cover the technical concept of autoencoders, their stacked variants, comparison with classical methods like PCA, and their practical application with Keras.

Theory of autoencoders: input reconstruction and traditional applications

An autoencoder is a neural network composed of two symmetrical parts: an encoder and a decoder. The encoder learns to compress the original input into a lower-dimensional representation, called the latent vector. The decoder tries to reconstruct the original input from this compressed vector. The training objective is to minimize the difference between the input and the reconstructed output.

The basic architecture consists of:

- an input layer
- one or more dense layers in the encoder
- a latent layer, with lower dimension than the original

- one or more dense layers in the decoder
- an output layer with the same shape as the input

This structure allows the network to discover internal representations of the data, especially useful in scenarios such as:

- image and signal compression
- noise removal (denoising autoencoders)
- visualization of high-dimensional data
- pretraining in unsupervised models
- detection of unusual patterns in large datasets

Keras allows direct construction of autoencoders using the Functional API. A basic model can be built as follows:

python

```python
from tensorflow.keras.layers import Input, Dense
from tensorflow.keras.models import Model

input_layer = Input(shape=(784,))
encoded = Dense(128, activation='relu')(input_layer)
encoded = Dense(64, activation='relu')(encoded)
latent = Dense(32, activation='relu')(encoded)

decoded = Dense(64, activation='relu')(latent)
decoded = Dense(128, activation='relu')(decoded)
output_layer = Dense(784, activation='sigmoid')(decoded)

autoencoder = Model(inputs=input_layer,
outputs=output_layer)
autoencoder.compile(optimizer='adam',
loss='binary_crossentropy')
```

This autoencoder receives 784-dimensional vectors (such as flattened 28x28 images), compresses them to 32 dimensions, and reconstructs the output. The binary loss function is used for inputs normalized between 0 and 1.

During training, the network receives no labels. It learns to map the input to itself. Once trained, the encoder can be extracted separately and used as a dimensionality reducer.

python

```
encoder = Model(inputs=input_layer, outputs=latent)
```

With this partial model, any new input can be converted into a compressed version, ideal for clustering, visualization, or preprocessing applications.

Stacked autoencoders: practical example for anomaly detection

Autoencoders can also be used to detect anomalies in data. Since the network learns the typical reconstruction patterns, inputs that deviate from these patterns will have significantly higher reconstruction errors. By measuring this error, it is possible to identify unexpected observations.

This process is especially useful in:

- financial fraud detection
- industrial sensor monitoring
- fault analysis in embedded systems
- disease diagnosis using standardized tests

For this, the model must be trained only with normal data. After training, the test data is passed through the autoencoder and the reconstruction is compared to the input. Inputs with reconstruction error above a threshold are considered anomalous.

The reconstruction error can be calculated using the mean of the squared differences:

python

```
import numpy as np

predictions = autoencoder.predict(x_test)
error = np.mean(np.square(x_test - predictions), axis=1)
```

The threshold can be defined based on percentiles, visual analysis, or empirical testing. A histogram of error distribution helps identify a suitable cutoff point.

python

```
import matplotlib.pyplot as plt

plt.hist(error, bins=50)
plt.xlabel("Reconstruction error")
plt.ylabel("Frequency")
plt.show()
```

Stacked autoencoders, which have several layers in both encoder and decoder, are especially effective in learning complex representations. They allow the network to capture hierarchical structures in the data, similar to the behavior of deep supervised networks.

Adding regularization such as Dropout, L2 penalties, and controlled noise improves the model's ability to generalize and prevents it from memorizing the input data.

Comparison with PCA: how classical approaches influenced deep networks

Before autoencoders, the main dimensionality reduction technique was Principal Component Analysis (PCA). PCA projects data onto orthogonal directions of maximum variance, reducing dimensions with minimal information loss. It is a linear, fast, and widely used technique.

Autoencoders can be seen as a nonlinear generalization of PCA. While PCA finds linear combinations of features, autoencoders, by using layers with nonlinear activation functions, are capable of capturing more complex patterns, curves, and highly distributed structures.

Main differences:

- PCA is linear; autoencoders are nonlinear
- PCA has an analytical solution; autoencoders require training
- autoencoders can be adapted to specific tasks
- PCA is less flexible but more interpretable

In practice, autoencoders outperform PCA when the data has strong nonlinear relationships, such as images, sounds, or biomedical signals. However, PCA is still valuable for quick exploratory analysis, initial noise reduction, or compression in tasks with lower complexity.

Common errors and solutions

Error: autoencoder output differs from input
Using incorrect activations or input scales outside the activation function range leads to poor reconstruction.
Solution: normalize data between 0 and 1 and use sigmoid activation in the output layer.

Error: autoencoder memorizes the data
When the model has too many layers or parameters, it learns to copy the data without generalizing.
Solution: reduce latent dimension, add Dropout, and use fewer neurons per layer.

Error: anomaly detection with many false positives
Poorly calibrated thresholds or noisy data can generate excessive alerts.
Solution: calculate the threshold based on reconstruction error percentiles in the validation set.

Error: model does not converge

Improper learning rate settings or activation functions cause stagnation.

Solution: try different optimizers like Adam, activate functions like ReLU in intermediate layers, and normalize the data.

Best practices and real-world applications

- normalize data before feeding it to the autoencoder
- use latent dimension smaller than 20% of the original dimension
- use symmetrical layers between encoder and decoder
- visually evaluate reconstruction in the case of images
- apply regularization to avoid overfitting
- combine with PCA as a comparison or initial reduction step

Autoencoders are widely used in:

- compression of medical images for efficient storage
- dimensionality reduction in clustering pipelines
- data preprocessing in complex networks
- anomaly detection in automated production systems
- noise reduction in sensor signals

In applications such as predictive maintenance, cybersecurity, and automated inspection, autoencoders offer a lightweight, unsupervised, and highly effective mechanism to capture behavioral deviations.

Autoencoders represent one of the most elegant and effective forms of unsupervised learning in neural networks. Their ability to compress data, identify patterns, and reveal internal structures makes them an indispensable tool in projects requiring dimensionality reduction, compression, or irregularity detection.

More than an alternative to PCA, autoencoders are a conceptual advancement, incorporating the ability to learn nonlinear representations tailored to the problem domain. They allow the model to understand its data without explicit labels, autonomously extracting useful information.

With the correct application of these techniques, it is possible to transform raw datasets into informative latent vectors, powering lighter, faster, and more accurate models. This is the power of learned representation – not just processing, but understanding data in depth.

CHAPTER 15 – GENERATIVE ADVERSARIAL NETWORKS (GANS)

Generative Adversarial Networks, known as GANs, have revolutionized the field of artificial intelligence by introducing a new paradigm of unsupervised learning: the competition between two neural networks to generate realistic synthetic data. This approach has enabled impressive advances in the generation of images, videos, audio, text, and even molecules. The base architecture of a GAN consists of two opposing networks—the generator and the discriminator—which are trained simultaneously with conflicting goals. The generator tries to deceive the discriminator, while the discriminator attempts to distinguish between real and synthetic data. This tension creates a refined learning environment in which the generator gradually learns to produce data that is nearly indistinguishable from reality.

Concepts of generator and discriminator: an overview of the initial GAN idea

The original proposal of GANs emerged from the observation that neural networks could be used not only for classification or prediction, but also for creation. Ian Goodfellow and colleagues proposed a structure composed of two neural networks trained in opposition. The generator network receives a random input vector (noise) and attempts to produce an output similar to real data. The discriminator network evaluates whether the received sample is authentic (from the real dataset) or fake (created by the generator).

This constant battle between the two networks creates a powerful learning dynamic, where both evolve together. The GAN becomes a tool that learns to generate synthetic data that follow the same distributions as real data, without needing to explicitly understand their internal structure.

The generator G tries to maximize the probability that the discriminator D will classify its outputs as real. The discriminator tries to minimize that probability, maintaining the ability to detect fakes. At the end of the process, the generator network learns to create samples so convincing that the discriminator can no longer distinguish them accurately.

Basic GAN architecture in Keras: step-by-step simple implementation

Building a GAN with Keras involves three main components: the generator network, the discriminator network, and the combination of both in an adversarial model. The first step is to build the generator. It transforms a noise vector into an image or sample with the same dimensions as the real data.

python

```
from tensorflow.keras.layers import Dense, LeakyReLU, Reshape
from tensorflow.keras.models import Sequential

def build_generator():
    model = Sequential()
    model.add(Dense(128, input_dim=100))
    model.add(LeakyReLU(alpha=0.2))
    model.add(Dense(784, activation='tanh'))
    model.add(Reshape((28, 28, 1)))
```

```
    return model
```

The 100-dimensional input vector is converted into a 28x28 image, like those in MNIST. The tanh function is used to keep the output values in the range [-1, 1].

Next, the discriminator is defined, which receives an image and returns a probability that it is real or fake.

python

```
from tensorflow.keras.layers import Flatten
from tensorflow.keras.models import Model

def build_discriminator():
    model = Sequential()
    model.add(Flatten(input_shape=(28, 28, 1)))
    model.add(Dense(128))
    model.add(LeakyReLU(alpha=0.2))
    model.add(Dense(1, activation='sigmoid'))
    return model
```

The discriminator is compiled separately with a binary loss function and an optimizer like Adam:

python

```
discriminator = build_discriminator()
discriminator.compile(optimizer='adam',
loss='binary_crossentropy', metrics=['accuracy'])
```

The generator is not trained on its own initially. It is incorporated into the adversarial model, where the discriminator is frozen (non-trainable) so that backpropagation affects only the generator's weights.

python

```python
from tensorflow.keras.models import Model
from tensorflow.keras.layers import Input

generator = build_generator()
noise_input = Input(shape=(100,))
generated_image = generator(noise_input)

discriminator.trainable = False
validity = discriminator(generated_image)

gan = Model(noise_input, validity)
gan.compile(optimizer='adam', loss='binary_crossentropy')
```

Training occurs in two cycles. First, the discriminator is trained with real data and fake images created by the generator. Then, the generator is trained through the GAN, with the discriminator frozen, forcing it to improve its forgeries.

python

```python
import numpy as np
```

```
def train(generator, discriminator, gan, real_data, epochs,
batch_size):
    half_batch = batch_size // 2
    for epoch in range(epochs):
        idx = np.random.randint(0, real_data.shape[0],
half_batch)
        real_images = real_data[idx]
        noise = np.random.normal(0, 1, (half_batch, 100))
        fake_images = generator.predict(noise)

        discriminator.trainable = True
        discriminator.train_on_batch(real_images,
np.ones((half_batch, 1)))
        discriminator.train_on_batch(fake_images,
np.zeros((half_batch, 1)))

        noise = np.random.normal(0, 1, (batch_size, 100))
        discriminator.trainable = False
        gan.train_on_batch(noise, np.ones((batch_size, 1)))
```

This process is repeated over several epochs. Over time, the quality of the generated images improves progressively.

Real-world applications: image synthesis, data augmentation, and other classic uses

GANs have become central tools in many technical and creative fields. Some classic applications include:

STUDIOD21 SMART TECH CONTENT

- **Realistic image generation:** used in the creation of synthetic human faces, landscapes, clothing, and objects. Models like StyleGAN generate images with surprising resolution and detail.
- **Data augmentation:** generate new synthetic samples to expand training datasets, especially in contexts where real data is scarce or sensitive.
- **Noise removal:** use GANs to clean corrupted images or reconstruct low-quality files.
- **Domain conversion:** transform images from one domain to another, such as photos to paintings (CycleGAN), maps to landscapes, or sketches to realistic images.
- **Deepfakes:** generation of realistic videos with faces or voices of people, with relevant ethical and legal implications.
- **Medical simulation:** generate synthetic scans for model training, such as MRIs or CT scans, while preserving privacy.

The ability to learn without labels makes GANs extremely valuable in areas with legal constraints, such as healthcare, or with high labeling costs.

Common errors and solutions

Error: generator always produces the same pattern
This issue, known as mode collapse, occurs when the generator finds one output that fools the discriminator and keeps repeating it.
Solution: apply strategies like batch discrimination, add noise to the discriminator, or use alternative loss functions such as Wasserstein loss.

Error: unstable training
GANs are notoriously difficult to train. Small performance

differences between networks cause loss of balance.

Solution: use optimizers with adjusted learning rates, techniques like label smoothing, and stable initializations.

Error: discriminator overpowers generator
When the discriminator learns too quickly, it rejects all generator outputs, blocking learning.
Solution: partially freeze the discriminator, apply regularization, or add noise to the inputs.

Error: loss does not reflect quality
GAN loss does not always indicate real progress. It may decrease without visible improvement in the generated samples.
Solution: save images at fixed intervals for visual inspection. Combine quantitative analysis with direct observation.

Best practices

- normalize input data between -1 and 1 when using tanh in the generator
- use LeakyReLU instead of ReLU to avoid inactive neurons
- balance training by alternating between discriminator and generator updates
- monitor outputs visually to track qualitative evolution
- experiment with different architectures to find balance between the networks

More robust models such as DCGAN, WGAN, LSGAN, and CycleGAN offer improvements in stability and performance for specific applications. These variants should be explored after mastering the basic architecture.

GANs represent one of the greatest innovations in the history of applied artificial intelligence. By combining algorithmic creativity with unsupervised learning, they expand the boundaries of what machines are capable of generating. With them, synthetic data play a central role in training, simulation, and creative processes.

More than a technique, GANs inaugurate a new way of thinking in AI: realistic simulation as a form of learning. By mastering this approach, the developer becomes able to create not only classifiers or predictors, but content generators, pattern replicators, and automated creative tools.

Adversarial networks show that learning to distinguish is also learning to create. And it is in this dialectic between truth and falsity that GANs produce their finest works.

CHAPTER 16 – NLP
OVERVIEW WITH KERAS

Natural Language Processing (NLP) enables machines to understand, interpret, and generate human language efficiently. With advancements in deep learning libraries, especially Keras, it has become feasible to implement high-performance NLP pipelines with practical applicability. Mastering this field involves fundamental steps such as tokenization, embeddings, and model architectures capable of handling textual sequences. In this chapter, we will cover the practical foundation of NLP in Keras, including text representation techniques, simple translation model construction, and an introduction to adapting Transformers within the framework.

Tokenization and embeddings: review of traditional techniques and use of Embedding layers

Natural language must be converted into a numerical format before being processed by neural networks. This transformation is done through tokenization, which divides text into smaller units such as words, subwords, or characters, and assigns each one an integer identifier.

Keras provides practical utilities for this process:

python

```
from tensorflow.keras.preprocessing.text import Tokenizer
from tensorflow.keras.preprocessing.sequence import pad_sequences
```

```python
texts = ["this is an example", "neural networks in NLP"]
tokenizer = Tokenizer(num_words=10000)
tokenizer.fit_on_texts(texts)

sequences = tokenizer.texts_to_sequences(texts)
inputs = pad_sequences(sequences, maxlen=10)
```

The resulting sequences are integer vectors representing the texts. Since words have meaning and semantic relationships, it's important that these representations are dense and vectorized in a continuous space. For this, we use embeddings.

The Keras Embedding layer transforms each integer token into a fixed-dimension vector. This vector representation is adjusted during training, allowing the model to capture semantic similarities:

python

```python
from tensorflow.keras.models import Sequential
from tensorflow.keras.layers import Embedding

model = Sequential()
model.add(Embedding(input_dim=10000, output_dim=64,
input_length=10))
```

Each word will be represented as a 64-dimensional vector. During supervised training, the embedding weights are adjusted to capture the language patterns specific to the problem.

Embeddings can also be loaded from pretrained vectors, such as GloVe or Word2Vec, offering a ready semantic base for tasks with limited labeled data.

Simple Seq2Seq models: introductory view of machine translation and chatbots

Sequence-to-sequence (Seq2Seq) models are used for tasks where both input and output are sequences, such as machine translation, text summarization, response generation, and speech transcription. These models are generally composed of two recurrent networks: an encoder and a decoder.

The encoder receives the input and generates a context vector, which condenses the meaning of the sequence. This vector is passed to the decoder, which generates the output sequence step by step.

In Keras, a simple implementation can be structured as follows:

python

```
from tensorflow.keras.models import Model
from tensorflow.keras.layers import Input, LSTM, Dense


# Encoder
encoder_input = Input(shape=(None,))
encoder_embedding = Embedding(10000, 64)(encoder_input)
encoder_output, state_h, state_c = LSTM(128,
return_state=True)(encoder_embedding)


# Decoder
decoder_input = Input(shape=(None,))
```

```
decoder_embedding = Embedding(10000, 64)(decoder_input)

decoder_lstm = LSTM(128, return_sequences=True)
(decoder_embedding, initial_state=[state_h, state_c])

output = Dense(10000, activation='softmax')(decoder_lstm)


seq2seq_model = Model([encoder_input, decoder_input],
output)

seq2seq_model.compile(optimizer='adam',
loss='categorical_crossentropy')
```

This model receives two inputs: the original sentence and the shifted target sequence (teacher forcing). It is capable of learning to map sentences from one language to another, answer questions, or maintain simple dialogues.

To train the model correctly, the data must be aligned between input and output, with consistent vocabulary and synchronized encodings.

Basic Transformers in Keras: initial adaptation of the classical structure in the framework

Transformers have replaced recurrent networks as the standard model for complex NLP tasks. Their ability to parallelize and learn long-range dependencies has made them the reference in modern architectures like BERT, GPT, and T5.

Keras, together with TensorFlow, provides layers and structures compatible with building Transformer-based models. The core of this architecture is the attention mechanism, especially self-attention.

The creation of a basic Transformer involves multiple steps but can begin with a simplified multi-head attention block:

python

```python
from tensorflow.keras.layers import MultiHeadAttention,
LayerNormalization, Dropout, Dense

def transformer_block(inputs):
    attention = MultiHeadAttention(num_heads=4,
key_dim=64)(inputs, inputs)
    attention = Dropout(0.1)(attention)
    output1 = LayerNormalization(epsilon=1e-6)(inputs +
attention)

    feedforward = Dense(256, activation='relu')(output1)
    feedforward = Dense(inputs.shape[-1])(feedforward)
    feedforward = Dropout(0.1)(feedforward)

    output2 = LayerNormalization(epsilon=1e-6)(output1 +
feedforward)
    return output2
```

This block can be stacked in encoder or decoder models, creating scalable architectures.

Transformers in Keras can be integrated with positional embedding layers, attention masks, and output heads for specific tasks such as classification, translation, or summarization.

Auxiliary libraries such as Hugging Face's transformers also allow loading ready-made models like BERT, GPT2, and T5 with full integration into the Keras ecosystem, offering a bridge between rapid development and production capability.

Common errors and solutions

Error: poorly prepared text inputs

Poorly configured tokenizers or unstandardized data generate inconsistent inputs and incoherent results.

Solution: use tokenizers with fixed vocabulary, apply pad_sequences with consistent truncation and padding.

Error: embeddings out of expected range

Models with Embedding layers do not train well when indices exceed the defined vocabulary.

Solution: set num_words according to the highest expected index. Check vocabulary size before compiling.

Error: misalignment in Seq2Seq models

Misaligned inputs and outputs prevent effective learning.

Solution: apply output data shifting and adjust indices with start and end of sequence tokens.

Error: transformer model does not converge

Transformers require more data and careful regularization.

Solution: use dropout, learning rate warm-up, layer normalization, and positional embeddings.

Best practices and real applications

- normalize and clean text before any tokenization
- use pretrained embeddings when possible to accelerate convergence
- keep vocabulary limited to the most frequent words to avoid noise

- train Seq2Seq models with teacher forcing and tune architecture with cross-validation
- use attention for tasks requiring context interpretation
- explore ready-made models like BERT for tasks such as sentiment analysis, entity extraction, and text classification

NLP applications with Keras range from recommendation systems and virtual assistants to legal analysis and medical processing. The ability to structure textual data into well-defined vector representations enables the construction of robust systems with direct impact on productivity and organizational intelligence.

Natural Language Processing with Keras offers a solid and accessible platform to transform human language into structured and actionable information. By understanding the fundamentals of tokenization, embeddings, Seq2Seq models, and Transformers, the AI professional becomes equipped to build powerful solutions applicable across multiple domains.

More than understanding text, modern NLP allows us to generate, interpret, summarize, and transform language into practical knowledge. And with Keras, this process becomes accessible, scalable, and integrated into the deep learning ecosystem. By mastering these tools, the developer becomes a builder of bridges between language and machine, between data and decisions.

CHAPTER 17 – DEBUGGING AND VISUALIZATION TOOLS

As deep learning models grow more complex, so does the need for robust observation and debugging mechanisms. During training, several elements can behave unexpectedly: stagnant metrics, oscillating loss, intensifying overfitting, weights that do not update, or layers that are not activated. Visualization tools allow real-time tracking of the network's internal behavior and enable more precise diagnostics. This chapter presents the main practical approaches to debugging and visual analysis using Keras and TensorFlow, focusing on strategic interpretation and reliable practices.

TensorBoard: monitoring metrics, neural network graphs, and weight histograms

TensorBoard is TensorFlow's official visualization dashboard, developed to monitor and analyze models interactively. It offers features such as loss and accuracy curve visualization, inspection of computational graphs, weight histograms, gradient distributions, embedding projections, and even generated images. Its integration with Keras is straightforward and efficient.

The first step is to create a callback that saves training logs:

python

```
from tensorflow.keras.callbacks import TensorBoard
import datetime

log_dir = "logs/training_" +
datetime.datetime.now().strftime("%Y%m%d-%H%M%S")
```

```
tensorboard_callback = TensorBoard(log_dir=log_dir,
histogram_freq=1)
```

This directory will store real-time metrics. The parameter histogram_freq=1 activates weight histogram capture per epoch. To include the callback in training:

python

```
model.fit(x_train, y_train, epochs=10, validation_data=(x_val,
y_val), callbacks=[tensorboard_callback])
```

With the log generated, the dashboard can be accessed via terminal:

bash

```
tensorboard --logdir=logs/
```

The interface displays loss and accuracy curves across epochs, facilitating analysis of underfitting and overfitting. Histograms allow evaluation of weight dispersion, detection of saturation, and identification of learning issues. The Graph tab enables navigation through the model's structure, inspecting connections and data flows.

TensorBoard also supports image visualization, such as input samples, activations, or generated outputs. This makes the diagnostic process visual, dynamic, and more aligned with human interpretation.

Custom logs: execution history logging using traditional logging practices

Beyond visual monitoring, event logging is essential for tracking executions, documenting tests, and reproducing experiments. Keras allows recording custom events via callbacks.

Using Python's logging library is a well-established practice that simplifies control of technical messages:

python

```
import logging

logging.basicConfig(filename='execution.log',
level=logging.INFO)
logging.info('Starting training with batch size 32')
```

During training, it's possible to capture statistics and log specific conditions:

python

```
class CustomLog(tf.keras.callbacks.Callback):
    def on_epoch_end(self, epoch, logs=None):
        acc = logs.get('accuracy')
        val_acc = logs.get('val_accuracy')
        logging.info(f'Epoch {epoch + 1}: acc={acc},
val_acc={val_acc}')
```

These logs provide a textual history that complements the visual dashboard. They are useful for auditing, version control, and comparing experiments.

Combining TensorBoard and manual logs allows you to observe trends, analyze patterns, and answer questions such as: when did overfitting begin? Which configuration yielded the best result? How many epochs were needed for convergence?

Activation visualization: interpreting intermediate layers and detecting issues

Understanding how the network responds to specific inputs is one of the most effective debugging methods. Intermediate layer activations reveal how data is being transformed throughout the network, indicating whether layers are being ignored, whether filters are learning, or whether saturation is occurring.

With Keras, it is possible to build partial models that return the outputs of specific layers:

python

```
from tensorflow.keras.models import Model

intermediate_layer = model.get_layer('dense_1')
activation_model = Model(inputs=model.input,
outputs=intermediate_layer.output)

output = activation_model.predict(x_test)
```

This output can be visualized as a matrix or converted into an image, depending on the task. In convolutional networks, observing activation maps shows which image regions influence the decision.

It is important to analyze whether:

- there are layers with near-zero activation
- activation maps are all similar (redundant filters)
- certain layers are saturated with maximum values

When activations do not change with different inputs, the network may be poorly initialized, poorly regularized, or learning irrelevant patterns. Inspecting these layers guides architecture and activation function review.

Another useful method is gradient visualization to detect vanishing or exploding gradients. Techniques such as Grad-CAM and saliency maps offer interpretable visualizations that help understand how decisions are made.

Common errors and solutions

Error: TensorBoard graphs not showing
Occurs when logs were not generated correctly or the directory is incorrect.
Solution: verify the path passed in log_dir and confirm that the callback is included in fit.

Error: overlapping old logs
Running multiple trainings in the same directory overwrites previous data.
Solution: create directories with unique timestamps for each run.

Error: layers with null output
Null activations indicate saturation or interrupted learning.
Solution: review activation functions, normalize data, and avoid poor initializations.

Error: incomplete logs
Poorly defined custom callbacks may fail to capture metrics properly.
Solution: implement callbacks with exception handling and null log checks.

Best practices

- use TensorBoard in all runs, even for prototypes
- save logs in directories organized by date and hyperparameters
- visualize activation maps in early and late layers
- capture custom logs accurately, avoiding overly verbose outputs
- store a snapshot of weights every N epochs for later analysis
- document hyperparameters along with logs to facilitate reproducibility

These practices not only help in identifying and correcting failures but also in justifying decisions, presenting results, and evolving the model with traceability.

Debugging and visualizing neural networks is more than fixing bugs – it is understanding how artificial intelligence is learning, making decisions, and evolving. Tools like TensorBoard, custom logs, and activation visualizations place the developer at the center of the process, enabling a strategic and technical reading of the model's internal behavior.

With these tools, the opacity of deep networks gives way to operational transparency. The developer begins to act as both scientist and engineer: observing, testing, correcting, and improving. The ability to interpret the network's signals is what distinguishes a model that merely works from one that truly performs. And this ability leads to the practical mastery of deep learning with confidence and control.

CHAPTER 18 – SAVING AND LOADING MODELS

Training a deep learning model requires time, computational resources, and technical expertise. Once the model reaches satisfactory performance, it is essential to reliably persist its weights and architecture. This not only preserves the work done but also enables reuse, environment transfer, result replication, version comparison, and integration with production pipelines. This chapter covers how to save models using Keras in standardized formats, recover structures and weights, apply technical versioning, and ensure stability in model reuse within real systems.

HDF5 and SavedModel formats: structure and how to persist weights and architecture

Keras offers two main ways to save models: the HDF5 format (.h5) and the SavedModel format, which is TensorFlow's recommended option for production. Both preserve not only the weights but also the model's architecture, optimizers, metrics, and training state.

To save a complete model in HDF5:

python

```
model.save('my_model.h5')
```

To load the saved model:

python

```
from tensorflow.keras.models import load_model
model = load_model('my_model.h5')
```

This format is efficient, portable, and widely accepted in various environments. Its internal structure organizes layers, weights, and parameters compactly, making it ideal for quick prototyping and collaboration.

The SavedModel format, on the other hand, is more robust for production and integration with TensorFlow Serving tools. It saves the model in a directory containing .pb files and subfolders with variables:

python

```
model.save('my_model_tf', save_format='tf')
```

And to load it later:

python

```
model = load_model('my_model_tf')
```

In addition to compatibility with TensorFlow Serving, this format allows the model to be loaded in different languages such as C++, JavaScript, and Swift, and deployed in environments with native support for TensorFlow Lite or TensorFlow.js.

If you want to save only the weights, Keras also allows this separately:

python

```
model.save_weights('weights.h5')
```

And to reload them:

python

```
model.load_weights('weights.h5')
```

This approach is useful when you want to manually reconstruct the architecture and only recover the trained parameters.

Traditional versioning techniques: valuing model versioning, metadata logs, and docstrings

Systematic model versioning is essential in machine learning engineering environments. This involves much more than numbering files. A good versioning system includes:

- standardized naming of files and folders with dates and identifiers
- storage of training hyperparameters
- capture of validation and test performance metrics
- logging of dependencies and libraries used
- documentation of changes in docstrings or README files

It is recommended to integrate technical logs directly into the saving cycle. A classic example of timestamp-based versioning:

python

```
import datetime
model.save(f'models/
model_{datetime.datetime.now().strftime("%Y%m%d_%H%M
%S")}.h5')
```

It is also common practice to generate a .json file containing metadata:

python

```python
import json

metadata = {
    'model': 'CNN for image classification',
    'training_date': str(datetime.datetime.now()),
    'epochs': 20,
    'optimizer': 'adam',
    'val_accuracy': 0.935
}

with open('models/metadata.json', 'w') as f:
    json.dump(metadata, f)
```

These records facilitate traceability, auditing, and version comparison, and support technical decisions on model improvement.

Model reuse in production: best practice for development teams seeking stability

Reusing trained models in production environments requires attention to critical aspects. The model must be exported cleanly, without unnecessary data, and accompanied by a well-defined inference interface.

When deploying a saved model, the engineering team must ensure:

- consistency between data preprocessing during training and in production
- version control of dependency libraries
- model isolation in containers or virtual environments
- unit testing of model inputs and outputs
- real-time performance monitoring

A well-established practice in production pipelines is creating a centralized loading function:

python

```python
def load_production_model(model_path):
    import tensorflow as tf
    model = tf.keras.models.load_model(model_path)
    return model
```

This function is called by APIs, microservices, or analysis scripts, ensuring that all systems use the same version of the model, avoiding inconsistencies.

In enterprise environments, model reuse also implies security and traceability. It is common to integrate model management solutions (MLflow, DVC, TFX) for full lifecycle control.

Common errors and solutions

Error: saved model fails to load correctly
When using custom layers, Keras may not recognize the structure upon loading.
Solution: register the custom layer using custom_objects in load_model.

Error: differences between training and production results
Divergent preprocessing between environments causes inference distortions.
Solution: encapsulate the data preparation pipeline into a unified function and share it with the team.

Error: version incompatibility

TensorFlow or Keras updates may break compatibility with saved models.
Solution: log the TensorFlow version at the time of saving and maintain controlled environments using requirements.txt or pip freeze.

Error: loss of metric history

Saving only weights or architecture prevents comparative performance analysis.
Solution: always save the training history (loss, accuracy, etc.) and store it alongside the model.

Best practices and real-world applications

- save complete models at the end of each relevant experiment
- use standardized naming with date, project name, and main metric
- document hyperparameters, datasets, and results along with the model
- prefer SavedModel format for production and compatibility with modern tools
- create automated scripts to save and load models at different pipeline stages
- always validate equivalence between saved and loaded

model

Integrate saving into callback logic for automatic checkpointing:

python

```
from tensorflow.keras.callbacks import ModelCheckpoint

checkpoint = ModelCheckpoint('best_model.h5',
monitor='val_accuracy', save_best_only=True)
```

In real projects, saving models is mandatory in:

- distributed training with multiple nodes
- hyperparameter tuning with cross-validation
- model comparison for A/B testing
- result replication in applied research
- integration with external systems via REST APIs or embedded services

Companies apply rigorous versioning to ensure reproducibility, production reliability, and regulatory audit readiness, especially in critical areas such as healthcare, finance, and autonomous transportation.

Saving and loading models strategically is one of the pillars of maturity in machine learning projects. It goes beyond technical persistence: it ensures stability, traceability, and efficiency throughout the applied intelligence lifecycle.

By adopting appropriate formats, disciplined versioning, and integration with production tools, the developer raises the reliability level of their solutions, reduces rework, and accelerates time-to-market. Mastering this practice is what transforms isolated experiments into scalable systems. And it is in this mastery that the future of applied AI is built with quality, security, and operational intelligence.

CHAPTER 19 – SCALING AND DISTRIBUTION

As deep learning models become more sophisticated and datasets grow larger, the ability to scale training and distribute the computational load becomes essential. Keras, integrated with TensorFlow, offers native support for execution on multiple GPUs, TPUs, and distributed clusters, allowing AI projects to advance efficiently and accurately even in high-demand computational scenarios. This chapter explores practical scaling strategies, configurations to leverage modern accelerators, and the fundamentals of distributed training for heterogeneous clusters.

Training on GPU and TPU: proper settings for modern machines

Graphics Processing Units (GPUs) have transformed deep learning by offering thousands of parallel cores for floating-point operations. When training a model with Keras, GPU usage is automatic if a CUDA environment is properly installed. TensorFlow detects the available GPU and moves tensors and operations to it without requiring changes to the original code.

To check if a GPU is being used:

python

```
from tensorflow.python.client import device_lib
print(device_lib.list_local_devices())
```

Or directly with TensorFlow:

python

```
import tensorflow as tf
print("Available GPU:", tf.config.list_physical_devices('GPU'))
```

TensorFlow allows explicit control over memory allocation:

python

```
gpus = tf.config.list_physical_devices('GPU')
tf.config.experimental.set_memory_growth(gpus[0], True)
```

This adjustment prevents the GPU from reserving all memory upfront, allocating memory on demand as execution progresses.

Tensor Processing Units (TPUs) offer even more performance at scale. They require integration with the Google Cloud environment or Colab, which provides TPUs for free. Code must be adapted for use with tf.distribute.TPUStrategy:

python

```
resolver = tf.distribute.cluster_resolver.TPUClusterResolver()
tf.config.experimental_connect_to_cluster(resolver)
tf.tpu.experimental.initialize_tpu_system(resolver)
strategy = tf.distribute.TPUStrategy(resolver)
```

```
with strategy.scope():
    model = build_model()
    model.compile(...)
```

Training on TPU can significantly accelerate the process, especially on high-dimensional datasets or deep architectures with many parameters.

Multi-GPU distribution: introduction to parallelism strategies in Keras

When multiple GPUs are available, Keras allows training to be parallelized using the MirroredStrategy, which replicates the model across all GPUs and synchronizes gradients at each step.

python

```
strategy = tf.distribute.MirroredStrategy()
```

```
with strategy.scope():
    model = build_model()
    model.compile(...)
```

This approach does not require changes to the model. Keras handles batch splitting across GPUs and gradient averaging. It is ideal for workstations with two or more local GPUs.

Other distribution strategies include:

- MultiWorkerMirroredStrategy: for training on multiple nodes with GPUs in each machine.
- ParameterServerStrategy: separates parameters into

dedicated servers and computations into workers.

- CentralStorageStrategy: keeps weights on the CPU and distributes only data to GPUs.

The strategy choice depends on infrastructure topology, model size, and required synchronization frequency.

Classic cluster scenarios: using distributed TensorFlow, traditional lessons from high-performance computing

Distributed computing is well established in fields like bioinformatics, physical simulations, and aerospace engineering. With the advancement of deep learning, clusters are now used to reduce training time from weeks to hours.

TensorFlow allows task distribution across machines using MultiWorkerMirroredStrategy. The environment must be configured with environment variables indicating each node's role:

bash

```
TF_CONFIG='{
  "cluster": {
    "worker": ["worker1:port", "worker2:port"]
  },
  "task": {"type": "worker", "index": 0}
}'
```

This configuration file must be present on each participating machine. The Python code remains the same:

python

```
strategy = tf.distribute.MultiWorkerMirroredStrategy()
```

```
with strategy.scope():
    model = build_model()
    model.compile(...)
```

This model scales horizontally, ideal for large datasets requiring true parallelism. It uses high-speed networks to synchronize gradients, ensuring consistent learning.

Classic lessons from high-performance computing also apply:

- minimize inter-node communication
- group operations to reduce overhead
- maximize cache memory efficiency
- avoid I/O bottlenecks

Using binary formats like TFRecord accelerates data reading in clusters, and asynchronous pipelines with tf.data enable parallel reading, transformation, and loading during training.

Common errors and solutions

Error: inefficient GPU use

The model continues using only the CPU despite GPU availability.

Solution: check correct installation of CUDA, cuDNN, and drivers. Confirm with tf.config.list_physical_devices.

Error: excessive memory allocation

At startup, the GPU allocates all available VRAM, causing conflicts with other processes.

Solution: use set_memory_growth(True) to avoid full immediate allocation.

Error: distribution strategy not respected

With multiple workers, training fails or does not synchronize properly.

Solution: correctly configure the TF_CONFIG variable and use infrastructure with reliable synchronization.

Error: performance loss

Distributed training is slower than single GPU training.

Solution: review the batch size (should be larger in distributed setups), check I/O bottlenecks, and avoid excessive synchronized calls.

Best practices and real applications

- always verify that the model is actually using the available hardware
- use MirroredStrategy for local projects with multiple GPUs
- prefer TPUStrategy when using Google Cloud or Colab with large batches
- store datasets in optimized formats such as TFRecord or HDF5
- combine tf.data with asynchronous preprocessing to feed the model without interruptions
- profile with tf.profiler to identify bottlenecks
- increase batch size proportionally to the number of GPUs
- save checkpoints with ModelCheckpoint to avoid progress loss in distributed systems
- automate worker restart with orchestration tools like Kubernetes or Apache Airflow

Real-world applications that benefit from scaling include:

- training computer vision models with millions of images
- language processing with large-scale Transformer-based models
- scientific simulations involving multiple variables and fine adjustments

- corporate solutions needing to accelerate model time-to-deployment
- applied research environments testing hundreds of hyperparameter combinations

Scaling and distributing model training is no longer a competitive advantage—it's a requirement in real projects. The ability to leverage GPUs, TPUs, and clusters defines the agility, precision, and feasibility of large-scale AI solutions.

By mastering parallelism strategies offered by Keras and TensorFlow, the developer becomes capable of building pipelines that evolve from local prototypes to enterprise-level distributed training. This not only accelerates execution time but also expands the capacity to explore deeper models, larger datasets, and more complex scenarios.

Mastering scaling ensures that artificial intelligence operates at its full potential, free from artificial limitations imposed by hardware. It is the act of transforming computational resources into real strategic advantage.

CHAPTER 20 – HYPERPARAMETER TUNING WITH KERAS TUNER

The definition of hyperparameters has always been a critical and delicate step in the development of deep learning models. Before automation, this process relied heavily on the programmer's intuition, trial and error, and exhaustive manual experimentation. Choosing the number of neurons, number of layers, learning rate, or activation function could determine the success or failure of a model. As deep learning libraries matured, tools like Keras Tuner emerged to make this process more intelligent, structured, and efficient. This chapter presents the importance of tuning, how to integrate Keras Tuner with Keras models, and how to systematically search for hyperparameter combinations that maximize model performance.

Importance of Hyperparameters: revisiting the manual process of the past

For many years, building neural networks relied almost exclusively on the developer's experience. Manual adjustments to parameters such as the number of units per layer, regularization rate, batch size, and learning rate optimization were made based on successive attempts. While educational, this process was inefficient and did not scale well.

The choice of hyperparameters directly influences the model's behavior:

- a learning rate that is too high can cause divergence

- an excessive number of neurons can lead to overfitting
- insufficient regularization harms generalization
- poorly combined activation functions inhibit gradient flow

With the diversity of possible configurations, the number of combinations grows exponentially. Automating this process ensures a more structured search for optimized architectures, reducing experimentation cost and allowing focus to remain on data quality and the practical application of the model.

Keras Tuner: automated parameter and architecture optimization

Keras Tuner is an official library for automatic hyperparameter search and tuning in Keras models. It supports different search algorithms, such as:

- RandomSearch: randomly samples parameter combinations
- Hyperband: optimizes time and performance with adaptive resource allocation
- BayesianOptimization: estimates which combinations are more likely to improve performance
- SklearnTuner: integrates scikit-learn optimizers

Installation can be done with:

bash

```
pip install keras-tuner
```

The basic structure for using Keras Tuner involves three steps:

1. Define a parametrizable model function
2. Choose the search algorithm

3. Run the tuning process and retrieve the best results

Example of model-building function:

python

```python
import keras_tuner as kt
from tensorflow.keras.models import Sequential
from tensorflow.keras.layers import Dense, Dropout

def construir_modelo(hp):
    modelo = Sequential()
    modelo.add(Dense(units=hp.Int('unidades_1', min_value=32, max_value=256, step=32),
                activation='relu', input_shape=(input_dim,)))
    modelo.add(Dropout(rate=hp.Float('dropout_1', 0.0, 0.5, step=0.1)))
    modelo.add(Dense(units=hp.Int('unidades_2', 32, 256, 32), activation='relu'))
    modelo.add(Dense(1, activation='sigmoid'))

    modelo.compile(
        optimizer='adam',
        loss='binary_crossentropy',
        metrics=['accuracy']
    )
    return modelo
```

With the function defined, choose an optimizer:

python

```
tuner = kt.RandomSearch(
    construir_modelo,
    objective='val_accuracy',
    max_trials=10,
    executions_per_trial=2,
    directory='tuning_resultados',
    project_name='modelo_classificacao'
)
```

And start the search process:

python

```
tuner.search(x_train, y_train, epochs=10,
validation_data=(x_val, y_val))
```

At the end, the best model can be retrieved:

python

```
melhor_modelo = tuner.get_best_models(num_models=1)[0]
```

This model comes already trained with the best-found hyperparameters, ready to be evaluated on test data or saved for production.

Tuning examples: adjusting number of neurons, layers, dropout rates

Keras Tuner offers different types of hyperparameters:

- hp.Int(): **defines an integer within a range**
- hp.Float(): **defines a decimal value with interval and step**
- hp.Choice(): **selects a value from a predefined list**
- hp.Boolean(): **enables or disables model components**

Below, a version with activation function and number of layers selection:

python

```python
def construir_modelo(hp):
    modelo = Sequential()
    for i in range(hp.Int('num_camadas', 1, 3)):
        modelo.add(Dense(
            units=hp.Int(f'unidades_{i}', 64, 256, step=64),
            activation=hp.Choice('ativacao', ['relu', 'tanh'])
        ))
    modelo.add(Dense(1, activation='sigmoid'))
    modelo.compile(
        optimizer='adam',
        loss='binary_crossentropy',
        metrics=['accuracy']
    )
    return modelo
```

This approach allows evaluation of how many hidden layers are ideal, how many units to use in each, and which activation function yields the best result.

Common errors and solutions

Error: overly broad search space
Defining very large ranges can make the search inefficient or consume excessive time.
Solution: restrict intervals based on prior knowledge or past metrics.

Error: overfitting during tuning
Running too many iterations without validation may lead to models overly fitted to the validation set.
Solution: use executions_per_trial greater than 1, create a robust data split, and validate with an external test set.

Error: inappropriate metric usage
Incorrectly choosing the optimization objective compromises results.
Solution: select metrics appropriate to the problem, such as val_accuracy, val_loss, val_auc.

Error: reusing tuning directory
Running two different processes in the same directory can corrupt results.
Solution: use unique project_name and directory for each experiment.

Best practices and real-world applications

- define a clear model function with well-named hyperparameters
- use Hyperband when runtime is a critical factor
- log tuner results for documentation
- always validate the best models on data not used in tuning
- store the winning hyperparameters for reuse in production
- apply tuning in separate blocks (architecture, regularization, optimizers)
- combine tuning with callback techniques like EarlyStopping and ReduceLROnPlateau

Hyperparameter tuning is especially useful in:

- projects with small datasets, where overfitting is frequent
- custom architectures with many structural decisions
- automated pipelines that require reproducibility
- commercial applications demanding maximum performance

Searching for better hyperparameters is one of the most direct ways to boost machine learning model performance. With Keras Tuner, this process gains speed, method, and depth, transforming trial and error into a systematic, auditable process integrated into the technical development cycle.

Mastering automated tuning allows professionals to explore more solutions in less time, respond quickly to production demands, and build optimized models from the start. It is a core skill for those seeking technical excellence with real, applicable results. By adopting this practice, the developer begins to design models with surgical precision, extracting the maximum potential from the chosen architecture.

CHAPTER 21 – MONITORING AND OBSERVABILITY

As deep learning models transition from research environments to production systems, the ability to monitor their operation in real time becomes indispensable. It is no longer enough for a model to perform well on test data. Its stability, predictability, and alignment with business goals must be ensured over time. Monitoring and observability are therefore foundational pillars of operational maturity in artificial intelligence. This chapter presents the fundamentals of observability applied to models in production, integrations with industry tools, and best practices for alerting, tracing, and rapid response to anomalies.

Business metrics and observability techniques: evolution from logs, traces, and dashboards

Observability goes beyond technical monitoring. It involves the continuous collection of signals that allow understanding the internal state of a complex system based on its external outputs. In machine learning systems, this includes:

- operational metrics (latency, throughput, memory and CPU usage)
- model metrics (accuracy, loss, cross-entropy, F1-score, AUC)
- business metrics (conversion rate, churn, cost per prediction, return on investment)

The combination of these three categories enables the evaluation not only of whether the model is functioning technically, but whether it is delivering value in its applied context.

In addition to metrics, the technical pillars of observability include:

- **logs:** chronological records of events, such as errors, exceptions, function calls
- **traces:** tracking of distributed calls, useful in microservice architectures
- **dashboards:** visual panels displaying metrics in real time

To capture this information, it is recommended to instrument the code with measurement points in strategic locations:

python

```python
import logging

logging.basicConfig(level=logging.INFO)
logging.info('Starting batch inference')
```

And send metrics to external systems such as Prometheus or Grafana:

python

```python
from prometheus_client import Gauge

accuracy_metric = Gauge('model_accuracy', 'Model accuracy in production')
accuracy_metric.set(0.914)
```

The adoption of these practices enables the diagnosis of performance degradation, identification of statistical drift, and prevention of silent failures.

Integration with market tools: APM (Application Performance Monitoring) systems

APM tools were developed to observe complex systems in real time, identifying bottlenecks, failures, and anomalies. When integrated into the machine learning pipeline, they provide an additional layer of operational control.

Main tools include:

- **Datadog:** provides dashboards, alerts, distributed tracing, and ML model support via specific SDKs
- **Prometheus:** open-source monitoring system with scraping-based collection and integration with Grafana
- **Grafana:** metric visualization platform used to build real-time dashboards
- **ELK Stack (Elasticsearch, Logstash, Kibana):** popular for log centralization and event analysis
- **Sentry:** excellent for capturing errors and alerting in inference APIs

Integrating Keras with APM tools generally involves instrumenting inference endpoints. A classic example with Flask:

python

```
from flask import Flask, request
import time

app = Flask(__name__)

@app.route('/predict', methods=['POST'])
def predict():
```

```
start = time.time()

input_data = request.json['input']

result = model.predict([input_data])

end = time.time()

duration = end - start

logging.info(f"Inference completed in {duration:.4f}
seconds")

return {'result': result.tolist()}
```

This log can be automatically sent to a response-time analysis tool. In modern architectures, each component of the pipeline —from preprocessing to the final response—is individually observed.

Alerts and best practices in production: failure prevention and traditional rollback in complex systems

Building effective alerts is one of the most direct ways to preserve the integrity of models in production. Alerts should not be generic or overly sensitive. They must be:

- based on metrics relevant to the business
- calibrated with realistic thresholds
- triggered by events that require human or automated action

Common examples include:

- sudden drop in accuracy below a specific threshold
- abrupt increase in inference latency
- class imbalance in recent predictions
- unexpected volume of null or corrupted inputs

Alerts should be integrated with team communication tools (Slack, email, PagerDuty) and documented in quick-response runbooks.

Additionally, a rollback mechanism must be in place. This may include:

- keeping the previous version of the model on standby
- using versioning with hash-based control
- adopting a fallback model based on rules
- encapsulating the model in versioned Docker containers

Traditional rollback does not eliminate the need for root-cause analysis but ensures operational continuity until the issue is properly diagnosed.

Common errors and solutions

Error: model keeps running but predictions lose meaning

This type of silent failure occurs due to changes in input data patterns, without any technical error.
Solution: implement input distribution monitoring and drift validation.

Error: lack of logs at critical points

Without visibility into the internal flow, diagnosing issues becomes impossible.
Solution: insert logs at all pipeline stages, including input, preprocessing, inference, and output.

Error: excessive alerts cause fatigue

Poorly calibrated alerts are ignored over time and become ineffective.
Solution: review thresholds based on historical time series and implement severity-based escalation

.Error: lack of model traceability in production

Not knowing which version is in use prevents comparison and rollback.

Solution: adopt formal versioning and include model metadata in all API calls.

Best practices and real-world applications

- define a minimum set of metrics for each model in production
- use tools like MLflow or Neptune.ai to log metadata and metrics
- integrate observability dashboards with orchestration tools (Airflow, Kubeflow)
- automate periodic health checks
- build automatic validation mechanisms with production data in batch
- adopt canary deployment logic to test new models on small subsets before full rollout

Companies operating with high volumes of real-time requests use observability to ensure SLA, mitigate reputational risks, and maintain control over model behavior in the field. Classic use cases include recommendation engines, fraud detection, and credit analysis, where undetected deviations can cause significant financial impact.

Monitoring machine learning models in production is a commitment to technical responsibility and operational continuity. Artificial intelligence, no matter how advanced, is subject to errors, drifts, and degradation. Observability enables transforming uncertainty into precise diagnostics and agile responses.

By adopting consolidated practices of logging, tracing, versioning, and alerting, AI professionals expand their field of view—ceasing to be mere model builders and becoming guardians of trustworthy intelligent systems. This is what differentiates experimental prototypes from real-world solutions that sustain businesses, critical operations, and continuous innovation.

CHAPTER 22 – MLOPS AND CONTINUOUS INTEGRATION

The advancement of artificial intelligence depends not only on good models but also on well-defined processes to deploy these models into production with quality, reliability, and traceability. MLOps, or Machine Learning Operations, emerges as the adaptation of traditional DevOps principles to the reality of intelligent systems, aiming to ensure that model development is integrated into the overall application lifecycle. This chapter explores the fundamentals of MLOps, highlights the importance of automated pipelines, and presents classic and modern strategies for continuous integration, testing, and reproducibility.

Classic development cycles: valuing the traditional DevOps and CI/CD model

DevOps transformed software development by combining development (Dev) and operations (Ops), breaking down silos and promoting automation, continuous integration (CI), continuous delivery (CD), and infrastructure as code. With the emergence of machine learning, these principles have been adapted to include elements such as data, model validation, experimentation, and drift monitoring.

The classic MLOps cycle follows a structure that values:

- automation of model testing and validation
- versioning of code, data, and models
- experiment reproducibility
- integration with production environments through CI/CD pipelines

- safe and versioned rollback of previous models

Unlike traditional software, machine learning introduces additional variables: data quality and volume, variability in results, and continuous knowledge evolution. Therefore, the cycle must account not only for code delivery but also for the delivery and monitoring of the trained model, its environment, and its artifacts.

Automated pipelines: connecting Keras with CI tools for training, testing, and deployment

To transform a Keras project into a complete MLOps pipeline, it is essential to automate steps such as training, testing, validation, model saving, deployment, and monitoring. Tools like GitHub Actions, GitLab CI, Jenkins, CircleCI, and Bitbucket Pipelines allow workflows to be executed on each commit to the repository.

The basic structure of a pipeline for Keras models may include:

- **step 1:** code validation with linting and unit tests
- **step 2:** execution of training scripts with controlled parameters
- **step 3:** validation with test set and defined metrics
- **step 4:** versioning and saving the model to an artifact repository
- **step 5:** automated deployment via API or container
- **step 6:** alert activation and continuous monitoring

An example using GitHub Actions:

yaml

```
name: Model Training and Deployment


on:
  push:
```

```yaml
    branches:
      - main

jobs:
  train-and-deploy:
    runs-on: ubuntu-latest
    steps:
    - name: Checkout code
      uses: actions/checkout@v2

    - name: Install dependencies
      run: |
        python -m venv venv
        source venv/bin/activate
        pip install -r requirements.txt

    - name: Train model
      run: |
        python treino_modelo.py

    - name: Deploy via API
      run: |
        curl -X POST http://api.example.com/deploy-model
```

This pipeline automatically runs training and starts deployment if training is successful. The treino_modelo.py script must contain all steps for preprocessing, modeling, and saving.

For storing and versioning models, it's recommended to use artifact repositories like MLflow, DVC, Weights & Biases, or even S3, GCS, and Azure Blob storage with hash-based control and metadata.

Experiment reproducibility: use of containers and immutable environments

Reproducibility is both a technical and ethical requirement in AI projects. A model is only trustworthy if it can be reproduced with the same results on any machine, with the same data and parameters.

To achieve this, one should adopt:

- isolated and immutable environments with Docker or Conda
- fixed library versions via requirements.txt or environment.yml
- saving hyperparameters and configuration in JSON or YAML files
- version control for data and artifacts using tools like DVC

An example Dockerfile for Keras projects:

dockerfile

```
FROM tensorflow/tensorflow:2.13.0


WORKDIR /app
COPY . /app


RUN pip install -r requirements.txt
```

```
CMD ["python", "treino_modelo.py"]
```

Building immutable images ensures that any pipeline—whether local, cloud-based, or on a cluster—has access to the same environment, eliminating unexpected variations.

Moreover, the use of Jupyter notebooks should be accompanied by exporting to .py scripts with version control to avoid inconsistencies caused by unordered cells or untracked edits.

Common errors and solutions

Error: model in production differs from locally tested model
Caused by differences in environment, versions, or data files.
Solution: use containers, virtual environments, and complete versioning of datasets.

Error: pipeline fails in external environments
Environment variables, permissions, or dependencies may be missing in CI.
Solution: document all dependencies and use tools like .env, dotenv, or CI platform Secrets.

Error: lack of validation before deployment
Models without technical or business validation may cause regressions.
Solution: create mandatory test steps with minimum metrics before allowing automated deployment.

Error: model goes into production without traceability
Lack of versioning prevents rollback or later comparison.

Solution: generate a unique ID for each model version, log it, and associate it with metrics, date, and configuration.

Best practices

- integrate the entire ML cycle into version-controlled repositories
- maintain CI pipelines clearly divided into stages
- adopt experiment tracking tools like MLflow or Neptune.ai
- automate model rollback in case of failure
- avoid untracked notebooks in production
- use commit hash as a universal identifier for models, data, and scripts
- prioritize automated tests before any deployment
- document architectural decisions and results in README files or docstrings in scripts

MLOps represents the maturity of machine learning systems. It goes beyond model creation, embracing software engineering practices, automation, security, and reproducibility. Integrating Keras into CI/CD pipelines is not just a technical decision, but a professional posture that ensures scalability and trust in the solution.

By mastering MLOps, the developer begins to operate as a true intelligence architect, capable of transforming models into services, experiments into products, and scripts into living systems. This is the path of modern AI engineering: reliable, traceable, automated, and integrated into the continuous value stream of organizations.

CHAPTER 23 – INTERPRETING DEEP LEARNING MODELS

As deep learning models become more sophisticated and capable of solving complex problems with high accuracy, the demand for transparency and understanding of how these decisions are made also increases. Interpretability, once considered secondary, has become central in critical domains such as healthcare, finance, and security. Understanding the inner workings of a neural network is an essential step to validate results, build trust, and meet regulatory requirements. This chapter explores the challenges of interpretability, presents practical techniques for visualizing input relevance, and discusses their impact on sensitive applications.

Interpretability challenges: how deep learning is often seen as a "black box"

Deep neural networks operate through thousands or millions of parameters automatically adjusted during training. These complex structures, composed of multiple nonlinear layers, are excellent at capturing patterns and subtle relationships in data. However, due to this complexity, they are often perceived as opaque systems, where it is difficult to understand why a particular prediction was made.

This problem is amplified when:

- the model makes critical decisions (credit approval, disease diagnosis, fraud detection)
- there is direct impact on people or regulated processes
- decisions must be justified to users, clients, or auditors

Lack of interpretability can lead to distrust, hinder adoption in strategic sectors, and even prevent deployment due to legal barriers. Therefore, the search for methods to explain model predictions has become a priority.

Interpretability is not limited to explaining correct outcomes. It is also important for:

- detecting bias in datasets
- identifying anomalous behavior
- auditing decisions and validating models before production
- improving models based on learned patterns

Saliency map visualization techniques: Grad-CAM, Integrated Gradients

Interpretation techniques based on saliency maps are mainly used in computer vision tasks, but their principles can also be adapted for tabular and textual data. The idea is to identify which parts of the input most influenced the model's prediction, highlighting the elements with the greatest weight in the final decision.

Grad-CAM (Gradient-weighted Class Activation Mapping)

Grad-CAM uses the gradients of the model's output with respect to the activations of a specific convolutional layer to generate heatmaps that indicate the most important regions of the image. This is especially useful in CNNs applied to image classification.

Basic flow:

- Choose the last convolutional layer of the model
- Compute the gradient of the prediction with respect to that layer's activations
- Perform a global average of the gradients
- Multiply the averaged gradients by the activations
- Apply ReLU and resize the map to the original image size

Code usage:

python

```python
import tensorflow as tf
import numpy as np
import cv2

def generate_gradcam(model, image, target_layer):
    grad_model = tf.keras.models.Model(
        [model.inputs],
        [model.get_layer(target_layer).output, model.output]
    )

    with tf.GradientTape() as tape:
        inputs = tf.cast(image, tf.float32)
        activations, output = grad_model(inputs)
        predicted_class = tf.argmax(output[0])
        loss = output[:, predicted_class]

    grads = tape.gradient(loss, activations)[0]
    weights = tf.reduce_mean(grads, axis=(0, 1))
    gradcam = np.zeros(activations[0].shape[0:2])

    for i, w in enumerate(weights):
        gradcam += w * activations[0][:, :, i]
```

```
gradcam = np.maximum(gradcam, 0)
gradcam = cv2.resize(gradcam.numpy(), (image.shape[2],
image.shape[1]))
gradcam /= gradcam.max()


return gradcam
```

This heatmap can be overlaid on the original image, making it possible to identify the model's focus when making a decision.

Integrated Gradients

This technique computes the average of gradients along a path between a reference input (e.g., a completely black image) and the actual input. It is useful to ensure that the explanation is sensitive to the actual presence of features in the input and avoids spurious interpretations.

Main steps:

- Define a baseline input
- Interpolate multiple points between the baseline and the real input
- Compute gradients for each point
- Integrate the gradients along the path

This approach is more robust than simple gradient methods as it adheres to mathematical properties like linearity and sensitivity.

Libraries such as Captum (for PyTorch) and tf-explain (for TensorFlow/Keras) offer optimized implementations of these techniques, ready to integrate with existing models.

Critical applications: healthcare, finance, and sensitive areas requiring detailed explanations

Interpretability is not a technical luxury but a practical requirement in many industries. Examples where detailed explanations are mandatory:

- **Healthcare:** a diagnostic model cannot merely indicate the presence of a pathology. It must show which region of the image contains the detected pattern, especially in medical imaging.
- **Finance:** automated credit systems must justify rejections based on auditable criteria, avoiding implicit bias against protected groups.
- **Insurance:** decisions on policy values or coverage acceptance require transparency, particularly in legal disputes.
- **Security:** surveillance systems with facial recognition must be auditable to prevent false positives in minority populations.
- **Law:** legal models that suggest sentencing or legal classifications need to provide justifications aligned with legal frameworks.

In all these contexts, explainability increases trust, facilitates institutional adherence, and allows compliance with laws such as LGPD and GDPR, which require the right to explanation for automated decisions.

Common errors and solutions

Error: blindly trusting saliency maps
Heatmaps may appear visually coherent but don't always reflect the model's internal logic.
Solution: validate with multiple techniques and test using controlled inputs (perturbation, region replacement).

Error: applying interpretation techniques out of context

Image-based methods are not always valid for text or tabular data.
Solution: choose techniques appropriate for the modality and model type.

Error: over-relying on explanation to justify model errors
Interpretability does not replace model quality. Explaining a wrong decision doesn't make it acceptable.
Solution: use explanations for continuous improvement, not as defense for poorly trained models.

Error: not validating the consistency of explanations
If the same input yields different explanations after minor irrelevant changes, there's fragility.
Solution: test the robustness of explanations with slightly modified inputs.

Best practices

- combine multiple techniques to obtain complementary explanations
- integrate visualizations into monitoring dashboards
- save heatmaps and gradients for future audits
- involve domain experts in validating interpretations
- automate coherence tests between explanations and predictions
- apply explainability from early development stages, not just at the end
- document the techniques used and the limitations of their interpretation

The era of opaque models is fading. Interpretability is not only a regulatory requirement but a technical and strategic differentiator. Knowing what a model has learned is just as important as the accuracy it achieves. Especially in critical contexts, transparency is what separates trustworthy solutions from invisible risks.

By mastering techniques like Grad-CAM, Integrated Gradients, and other explainability approaches, AI professionals qualify to build more ethical, auditable, and sustainable systems. Intelligence should not just work. It should be explainable. And it is this capability that elevates artificial intelligence from experimental to essential.

CHAPTER 24 – INTEGRATION WITH OTHER LIBRARIES

The power of Keras is enhanced when combined with other fundamental libraries in the Python ecosystem. Its ability to integrate with tools like Scikit-Learn, Pandas, Matplotlib, and Plotly transforms Keras into a flexible operational core for machine learning projects. From data preparation to result visualization, these integrations provide flow and control to professionals seeking technical precision with real-world applicability. This chapter presents how Keras connects with major ecosystem libraries, offering a practical workflow that values each stage of a complete project.

Scikit-Learn and Pandas: feature preparation and engineering before feeding into Keras

The foundation of any machine learning model starts with data quality. Pandas is the most popular tool for manipulating, cleaning, and transforming datasets. Scikit-Learn, in turn, offers a solid collection of transformers, encoders, and data validators essential for feature engineering.

A typical integration flow between Pandas, Scikit-Learn, and Keras starts with reading the data:

python

```
import pandas as pd

data = pd.read_csv('clients.csv')
```

Then, traditional transformations can be applied:

python

```
# Replace missing values
data.fillna(0, inplace=True)
```

```
# Encode categorical variables
data = pd.get_dummies(data, columns=['gender',
'marital_status'])
```

```
# Normalize with Scikit-Learn
from sklearn.preprocessing import StandardScaler
```

```
scaler = StandardScaler()
data[['income', 'age']] = scaler.fit_transform(data[['income',
'age']])
```

After preprocessing, the data can be split into input and output to feed a Keras model:

python

```
X = data.drop('default', axis=1).values
y = data['default'].values
```

This continuous flow avoids reinventing steps and allows reuse of established code in pipelines that leverage the robustness of traditional libraries.

Another important point is the ability to package preprocessing with the model in a Scikit-Learn pipeline:

python

```
from sklearn.pipeline import Pipeline
from tensorflow.keras.wrappers.scikit_learn import
KerasClassifier
```

```
def create_model():
    from tensorflow.keras.models import Sequential
    from tensorflow.keras.layers import Dense
    model = Sequential()
    model.add(Dense(64, activation='relu',
input_shape=(X.shape[1],)))
```

```
   model.add(Dense(1, activation='sigmoid'))
   model.compile(optimizer='adam',
loss='binary_crossentropy', metrics=['accuracy'])
   return model

pipeline = Pipeline([
   ('scaler', StandardScaler()),
   ('classifier', KerasClassifier(build_fn=create_model,
epochs=10, verbose=0))
])
```

This facilitates cross-validation and integration with tools like GridSearchCV for hyperparameter tuning.

Plotting tools: Matplotlib and Plotly to monitor performance and loss

Visualizing training results is one of the most effective ways to detect problems early, understand model behavior, and adjust architecture or regularization decisions.

Matplotlib remains one of the most reliable tools to quickly generate statistical plots:

python

```
import matplotlib.pyplot as plt

history = model.fit(X_train, y_train, validation_data=(X_val,
y_val), epochs=20)

plt.plot(history.history['loss'], label='Training Loss')
plt.plot(history.history['val_loss'], label='Validation Loss')
plt.xlabel('Epoch')
plt.ylabel('Loss')
plt.legend()
plt.title('Loss Curve')
plt.show()
```

For interactive visualizations and more dynamic analysis, Plotly stands out. It allows zooming, navigation, and capturing deeper visual insights:

python

```
import plotly.graph_objs as go
from plotly.offline import iplot

fig = go.Figure()
fig.add_trace(go.Scatter(y=history.history['accuracy'],
name='Training Accuracy'))
fig.add_trace(go.Scatter(y=history.history['val_accuracy'],
name='Validation Accuracy'))
fig.update_layout(title='Accuracy per Epoch',
xaxis_title='Epochs', yaxis_title='Accuracy')
iplot(fig)
```

Both libraries can be used complementarily. The key is to ensure model performance is always visible for analysis, facilitating continuous adjustment and iterative improvement.

Examples of complete workflow: using Jupyter for integrated experiment notebooks

Jupyter notebooks remain a solid choice for exploratory experiments and hypothesis validation. **Their structure allows:**

- switching between data visualization and code
- executing cells individually for quick tests
- documenting reasoning throughout the process
- sharing knowledge with technical and business teams

A complete and well-structured notebook flow may include:

- Dataset import and description
- Preprocessing with Pandas and Scikit-Learn
- Initial visualizations with Matplotlib
- Model building and training with Keras
- Learning curve visualization
- Final evaluation on test set
- Model export and report generation with metrics
- Result interpretation with Grad-CAM or SHAP

Such documents are useful for both internal control and presentation in technical committees and business alignment meetings.

Common errors and solutions

Error: inconsistency between training and production data
This often occurs when data undergoes different preprocessing in production.
Solution: integrate preprocessing into the model pipeline or serialize transformers with joblib.

Error: loss of data metadata during transformation
Using .values or .to_numpy() drops column names, making tracking difficult.
Solution: keep Pandas structures until the last possible moment before feeding the model.

Error: type or format incompatibility between libraries
Transformations made in Pandas may generate objects incompatible with TensorFlow/Keras.
Solution: explicitly convert data with astype(np.float32) and validate dimensions.

Error: inaccurate or misinterpreted plots
Confusing loss curves with overfitting when the model is still learning.
Solution: use coherent scales, clear titles, and analysis based on quantitative reasoning, not just visuals.

Best practices and real-world applications

- keep the data pipeline external to the model, but versioned alongside it

- document each transformation with docstrings or markdown in Jupyter
- combine Pandas and Scikit-Learn for data validation and consistency
- use Keras callbacks to log metric history to external files
- include visualizations in the validation process to detect outliers and noise
- save notebooks in Git repositories with relevant checkpoint commits
- integrate model metrics with interactive visualizations to facilitate presentations

Projects where these practices are critical include medical diagnostics with convolutional networks, churn prediction with tabular data, and risk analysis in banking credit. In all these cases, coordinated use of classic libraries with Keras offers speed, clarity, and adaptability for different demands.

The strength of Keras lies in its simplicity and integrability. Combining Pandas, Scikit-Learn, Matplotlib, and Plotly in a unified flow enables machine learning professionals to create complete solutions grounded in solid data engineering and continuous visual validation. It's not just about training models, but about building reliable and traceable systems.

By mastering this integration, the developer gains not only productivity, but also the ability to create technical narratives that resonate with various business areas. Each graph, metric, and transformation becomes evidence of the value that applied intelligence can offer, from experiment to real-world impact.

CHAPTER 25 – ADVANCED DEPLOYMENT OF KERAS MODELS

Transforming a trained model into an accessible, scalable, and secure application is the decisive step that connects data science to tangible value generation. Deploying Keras models involves much more than just saving weights and loading files. It is about integrating the model into a service that can handle external requests, respond with low latency, and operate stably even under variable load. This chapter presents advanced strategies for deploying Keras-developed models, focusing on the creation of REST APIs, use of cloud serverless services, and the application of classical software engineering principles to achieve scalability and fault tolerance.

Serving models: REST API and traditional servers, recalling the use of FastAPI and Flask

The first step in deploying a Keras model is to transform it into a service that can receive inputs via HTTP and return predictions in real time. This is traditionally done through a REST API that encapsulates the trained model and exposes an endpoint for external calls.

Flask and FastAPI are lightweight and popular frameworks that allow this integration with ease. FastAPI, in particular, offers explicit typing, automatic validation, and superior performance, making it ideal for modern services.

Implementation with FastAPI:

python

```
from fastapi import FastAPI
from pydantic import BaseModel
import tensorflow as tf
import numpy as np


app = FastAPI()
model = tf.keras.models.load_model('modelo_final.h5')


class Input(BaseModel):
    features: list


@app.post("/predict")
def predict(data: Input):
    input_data = np.array([data.features])
    prediction = model.predict(input_data)
    return {"result": prediction.tolist()}
```

This service can be run locally with the command uvicorn filename:app --reload or packaged into a Docker container for more controlled environments. The use of standardized input formats such as JSON facilitates integration with external systems and reduces friction when consuming the API.

For heavier models or those with specific requirements, preprocessing and postprocessing can be included within the endpoint function itself, ensuring the API encapsulates the entire required flow.

Serverless and cloud: AWS Lambda, GCP Functions, or Azure Functions

Serverless environments offer the advantage of automatic scaling, reduced idle costs, and no need to manage infrastructure. For projects with sporadic usage or those that need to scale on demand, this architecture is ideal.

On AWS, the model can be saved in S3 and the Lambda function code configured to load it on demand. However, package size and execution time limits must be considered.

Flow with AWS Lambda:

- Save the model in S3
- Create a Lambda function with the loading and prediction code
- Configure an API Gateway to expose the function as an HTTP endpoint
- Adjust IAM permissions to allow access to the S3 bucket
- Monitor via CloudWatch for performance analysis

The code inside the Lambda function should optimize load time and favor in-memory storage whenever possible:

python

```
import boto3
import tensorflow as tf
import numpy as np
import json


model = None


def load_model():
```

```
global model
if model is None:
    model = tf.keras.models.load_model('/tmp/modelo.h5')

def lambda_handler(event, context):
    load_model()
    input_data = json.loads(event['body'])['features']
    prediction = model.predict(np.array([input_data]))
    return {
        'statusCode': 200,
        'body': json.dumps({'result': prediction.tolist()})
    }
```

This model can be adapted for Google Cloud Functions and Azure Functions with minor syntactic changes. The main advantage of the serverless model lies in its elasticity: you pay only for execution time, and the system scales automatically according to demand.

Scalability and fault tolerance: valuing classical software design practices for continuous robustness

In production environments, models do not operate in isolation. They are embedded in pipelines, interdependent services, and critical processes. To ensure these models operate with high availability, classical software engineering principles must be applied and adapted to the machine learning context.

Essential practices:

- redundancy: keep replicas of the model in different availability zones

- timeout and retries: avoid blocking with retry policies and time limits per call
- circuit breakers: stop calls to unstable services to avoid failure propagation
- model version control: ensure multiple versions can coexist and be tested in parallel
- blue-green deployment: implement new versions in parallel with the old one, with controlled switching
- canary testing: test a new version with a fraction of real traffic before scaling

In addition, continuous monitoring with metrics such as latency, memory usage, error rate, and prediction integrity is vital for early problem detection. Tools like Prometheus, Grafana, Sentry, and DataDog should be integrated from the beginning.

Common errors and solutions

Error: API with very high response time
Large models and real-time loading may cause excessive latency.
Solution: initialize the model outside the prediction function, use efficient serialization, and evaluate optimization with TensorFlow Lite.

Error: error when handling unexpected inputs
External users may send incomplete, poorly formatted, or out-of-domain data.
Solution: implement input validation with explicit typing, tests, and clear error messages.

Error: server overload with multiple simultaneous requests
Services without throttling or configured scaling may collapse.
Solution: configure processing queues, use auto-scaling or

serverless architecture.

Error: lack of versioning and rollback
Deploying a new version without validation or control can compromise operations.
Solution: use version tags, continuous integration pipelines, and metadata-controlled deployment.

Best practices

- use Docker containers to ensure portability across environments
- configure structured logging to facilitate later analysis
- integrate automated regression tests before deployment
- validate predictions with real data before production activation
- maintain fallback with simple rules in case the model becomes unavailable
- log all requests and responses in databases like MongoDB or BigQuery
- avoid hardcoded paths or parameters by using environment variables
- use external storage for artifacts and avoid embedding models in the main repository

Deployment is not the end of a model's journey, but the beginning of its operational responsibility. Turning a Keras model into a reliable, available, and auditable service requires attention to technical detail and adherence to best practices in systems engineering. Applied intelligence must operate with the same robustness as a banking, healthcare, or logistics system.

By mastering advanced deployment strategies, the machine learning professional extends their role from the lab to the frontline of intelligent systems. From promising prototypes to real-world applications, every line of deployment code is a bridge between science and real impact. And it is this well-built bridge that sustains trust in artificial intelligence at scale.

FINAL CONCLUSION

The journey we have taken throughout this book intertwines two fundamental aspects of the data science and machine learning ecosystem: the consolidation of Keras as a framework for developing deep neural networks and the continued relevance of Scikit-Learn as a foundation for tasks such as classification, regression, clustering, and data preprocessing. Although the focus of this work is the practical application of Keras, it is impossible to ignore that its value is amplified when combined with data manipulation and analysis libraries such as Pandas, visualization tools like Matplotlib and Plotly, and, above all, established modeling and validation solutions like Scikit-Learn.

Reflecting on the importance of mastering Scikit-Learn for data science essentially means understanding that deep learning does not operate in an algorithmic vacuum. It benefits from a data preparation, validation, and analysis pipeline that, for many years, has been structured by the concepts and methods of traditional libraries. Scikit-Learn provides transformers, validators, metrics, and workflows that, even in the face of the most advanced neural networks, remain crucial for the success of a project. Whether through cross-validation, variable normalization, dimensionality reduction, or as a quick baseline method, Scikit-Learn retains its prominence in the formation of a complete data science professional.

The synergy between these two approaches—the logic-based foundation of data manipulation and validation inherited from Scikit-Learn, and the expressive power of deep neural networks implemented in Keras—forms the core of a robust pipeline capable of handling highly complex scenarios. In many projects, the practitioner begins by manipulating the dataset with Pandas, applies transformations or feature selections with Scikit-Learn, and only then introduces Keras for the deep model construction phase, taking advantage of callbacks, functional APIs, and specialized architectures. The result is a cohesive workflow in which each library plays its best role, minimizing rework and maximizing results.

With this in mind, it is worth revisiting the sequence of chapters that composed this book, "LEARN KERAS – Master Neural Networks and Deep Learning with Python," outlining the key concepts and the relevance of each stage in shaping an autonomous AI professional capable of tackling real-world challenges.

Chapter 1 established the historical background of Keras, its philosophy of simplicity, and how it differs from other libraries such as PyTorch and pure TensorFlow. This starting point contextualized the decision to use Keras, emphasizing its creation to make neural network development accessible, with clean syntax and a focus on rapid experimentation. This differentiator proves essential in scenarios where prototyping speed and code clarity directly impact the adoption of machine learning solutions.

Next, Chapter 2 addressed environment setup and configuration, which is the initial step for any AI developer. Ensuring that Python, TensorFlow, and Keras function correctly enables subsequent projects to proceed smoothly. Additionally, organizing directories, defining virtual environments, and adopting version control practices prevent dependency conflicts. Though seemingly trivial, this stage establishes the foundation for a sustainable development pipeline, naturally integrating with data manipulation and preprocessing tools rooted in the Scikit-Learn ecosystem.

In Chapter 3, the theoretical foundations of neural networks came into play. It reviewed artificial neuron concepts, dense layers, activation, and historical evolution, highlighting how the field of deep learning emerged from the early days of the perceptron. For readers familiar with Scikit-Learn, it is interesting to note the similarities between logistic regression and the structure of a dense layer, or how the loss function and gradient descent appear repeatedly across various machine learning algorithms.

Chapter 4 introduced the Sequential model in Keras, demonstrating the simplicity of building dense networks and evaluating them on concrete problems. It explored functions such as fit(), compiling a model, and adjusting essential parameters such as the optimizer, loss function, and evaluation metrics. Those already proficient in Scikit-Learn find Keras to be a natural extension of concepts: while in Scikit-Learn one configures a Classifier or Regressor, in Keras the idea is to compile a network by defining the loss function, optimizer, and metrics. The coherence and fluency of the Python ecosystem are strongly manifested in this transition.

Chapter 5 delved into optimization algorithms and loss functions. Readers learned how Adam, RMSprop, SGD, and other approaches update weights, as well as the importance of selecting losses such as binary_crossentropy, categorical_crossentropy, or mean_squared_error according to the problem's nature. This knowledge echoes the model validation and parameter search principles observed in Scikit-Learn, where the choice of loss function and optimizer significantly impacts final performance. The ability to interpret and compare different optimization strategies is an integral part of AI proficiency.

Chapter 6 transitioned into convolutional architectures, CNNs, which revolutionized computer vision. Readers were invited to create Conv2D layers, apply pooling, and understand how padding affects activation maps. Although focused on images, this chapter reinforced the need to handle data in suitable structures, often preceded by a preprocessing and normalization pipeline—an area where Scikit-Learn excels with its transformers and modular pipelines.

Chapter 7 covered recurrent neural networks (RNNs), emphasizing the importance of handling sequential or temporal data. RNN, LSTM, or GRU models benefit from carefully crafted features, once again highlighting the synergy with external tools: the extraction and manipulation of time series or sequential records are efficiently handled by Pandas, Scikit-Learn, and, in more complex cases, specialized frameworks. Each chapter reinforces the need for an integrated ecosystem to handle data in various formats.

Chapters 8 and 9 presented the evolution from traditional RNNs to LSTM and GRU, along with additional training control elements such as callbacks, model saving, and learning rate scheduling. Callbacks, for instance, allow early stopping, validation checks, learning rate adjustments, and metric monitoring during fit execution. There is a conceptual resemblance to Scikit-Learn pipelines, where transformation, parameter tuning, and validation steps are separated—but here, the orchestration is internal to the neural network process. Readers realize that, whether using dense, convolutional, or recurrent networks, the pipeline becomes even more robust when the Scikit-Learn mindset for validation and testing is integrated.

Chapter 10 further explored regularization concepts: Dropout, Batch Normalization, and L1/L2 penalties are methods for preventing the model from merely memorizing the training set. This topic also resonates in Scikit-Learn, where regularization methods like Lasso and Ridge are used for linear regression problems. Neural network architecture, combined with overfitting control best practices, defines generalization capability—an essential concept in all of data science, regardless of the specific algorithm.

Chapter 11 addressed preprocessing and data augmentation. This is an area where synergy with libraries such as Pandas and Scikit-Learn becomes tangible: preparing tabular data, normalizing variables, synthetically augmenting datasets, or handling text all benefit from structured workflows and modular transformers. The essence of a robust pipeline involves managing every step of cleaning, selection, and information enrichment to feed Keras properly.

Chapter 12 introduced the Functional API and Model Subclassing. These Keras variations go beyond the limitations of Sequential, allowing networks with multiple inputs, outputs, internal merges, and branching. For multimodal or highly complex problems, this feature becomes essential. Here, too, the importance of well-structured projects is evident, as data flow complexity may mirror that seen in Scikit-Learn modular pipelines but with a greater emphasis on neural paths and layer combinations.

Chapter 13 introduced Transfer Learning as a way to leverage pretrained networks. This method directly relates to knowledge reuse strategies, useful in Scikit-Learn when stacking transformations or combining estimators in pipelines. The idea of freezing layers and performing fine-tuning shows how deep learning aligns with the principle of not reinventing the wheel when robust models for image, text, or speech already exist.

Chapter 14 explored autoencoders and dimensionality reduction, connecting to the world of PCA and other compression techniques in Scikit-Learn. The main difference is that while PCA is linear, autoencoders can capture non-linear relationships, approaching reconstruction and encoding problems for complex data. The synergy remains evident: those skilled in Scikit-Learn data manipulation pipelines find it easy to insert an autoencoder as an intermediate feature extraction step.

Chapter 15 introduced GANs (Generative Adversarial Networks), broadening the range of applications. GANs are revolutionary in synthetic data generation and creative tasks. Their development benefits from validation scripts and dataset manipulation that, while not native to Scikit-Learn, can be strengthened by integrating transformers for tabular data if preprocessing of features or labels is required.

Chapter 16 expanded Keras usage for NLP (Natural Language Processing), covering embeddings, tokenization, and seq2seq. Transitioning to text manipulation, with subwords or tokens, revisits essential data handling concepts supported by Pandas for organizing corpora and Scikit-Learn transformers for possible encodings. The pipeline mindset continues, and integrating this flow ensures technical robustness.

Chapter 17 introduced debugging and visualization tools, such as TensorBoard. Although specific to neural networks, this aligns with the data science mindset that values experiment tracking and a deep understanding of model evolution across epochs. In traditional machine learning scenarios, the equivalent would be analyzing logs and cross-validation reports. The difference is that, in deep learning, architecture complexity calls for specific tools to visualize activations and weight distributions.

Starting in Chapter 18, the focus shifted to practical application in production environments. The importance of saving and loading models, ensuring reproducibility and versioning, is well known in the Scikit-Learn community through model serialization with joblib and pipelines. In the Keras world, however, this becomes even more critical due to the size of weight files and the need for compatibility with specific TensorFlow versions.

Chapter 19 covered scaling and distribution, addressing training on GPU, TPU, and clusters, while Chapter 20 explored Hyperparameter Tuning with Keras Tuner. These topics demonstrate how deep learning reaches professional levels, requiring orchestration of powerful computational resources and automated tuning. The counterpart in the Scikit-Learn world would be parameter search via GridSearchCV or RandomizedSearchCV. The principle remains the same: systematizing experiments to find optimal configurations based on solid metrics.

Chapters 21 and 22 emphasized monitoring, observability, and MLOps. The idea of integrating CI/CD pipelines, well known in DevOps, is extended to models that evolve, receive different data, and require drift detection. Consolidating logs, metrics, and alerts aligns with Scikit-Learn best practices, which have always emphasized rigorous validations, but now elevates that rigor to an AI production environment where failures can result in economic, reputational, or regulatory risks.

Chapter 23 addressed model interpretability, presenting techniques such as saliency maps and Grad-CAM. Once again, the need to understand why a network made a given decision is not exclusive to Keras or deep learning. Interpretability methods exist in Scikit-Learn—such as feature importances in random forests or linear regressions—but in neural networks, the underlying complexity requires specific approaches that reveal where the model's attention was focused.

Chapter 24 showcased integration with libraries like Pandas, Matplotlib, and Scikit-Learn, demonstrating the power of a unified ecosystem. This chapter, in particular, reinforces the message that Keras is not isolated; it is part of a toolset that significantly enhances project productivity and clarity. The stitching together of data manipulation, modeling, visualization, and evaluation becomes natural when Scikit-Learn is mastered for preprocessing, Keras for deep modeling, and plotting libraries for final analysis.

Finally, Chapter 25 covered advanced deployment of models, discussing REST APIs, serverless architectures, and scalability best practices. This final phase is where all elements of data science converge: the data manipulation and validation pipeline (Scikit-Learn and Pandas) prepares the data, the Keras model performs prediction logic, and the deployment system ensures availability, performance, and reliability. It is the culmination of a well-structured project where each prior chapter finds its practical application.

This synthesis results from a carefully planned progression, following the TECHWRITE 2.1 Protocol, which aims to unite theory and practice in a balanced way, with no gaps or redundancies. Each chapter covers key concepts and tested examples, describes common errors and solutions, and recommends best practices in software engineering and data science. For those coming from the Scikit-Learn world, the transition to Keras becomes intuitive, as many conventions—such as separating training and validation data, measuring accuracy or F1 metrics, and systematically adjusting hyperparameters—are maintained, even though each library has its own specifics.

This entire journey highlights the importance of mastering Scikit-Learn as a foundation for data science. It not only complements Keras but supports the pipeline of data manipulation, exploration, and preparation that feeds deep neural networks. It is a fundamental link between the initial phase of statistical analysis and the implementation of sophisticated models. In-depth knowledge of Scikit-Learn routines and fluency with transformers, validators, and pipelines helps build integrated solutions where deep learning becomes just one component of an analytical and modeling ecosystem.

As we conclude this book, the message remains that true mastery in AI does not arise from algorithmic isolation. It comes from the ability to navigate through different layers of data engineering, understand the spectrum of linear and non-linear techniques, and articulate classical and modern tools in real-world projects. Keras provides accessibility and expressive power for neural networks, while Scikit-Learn provides the technical framework for tasks ranging from feature selection to extensive validation. Together, they form the foundation of a consistent applied machine learning practice, where the professional is not limited to a single approach but chooses, integrates, and customizes methods according to the problem's needs.

The hope is that each reader, throughout these chapters, has developed a greater sense of autonomy and confidence to face practical challenges in the field of deep learning. From building dense neural networks, through convolutions and recurrences, to transfer learning, autoencoders, GANs, and MLOps, the reader has gone through a progressive training that encompasses theoretical concepts and operational strategies. Each topic was enriched with tips, examples, and reflections on common mistakes and appropriate corrections.

It is important to recognize that the path of machine learning is dynamic. Libraries evolve, new architectures and regularization methods emerge, and the community frequently introduces innovative frameworks or paradigms. However, mastering the fundamentals—network architectures, activation functions, optimization, regularization, pipelines, and validation—remains the unshakable foundation that enables any developer, data scientist, or researcher to adapt to these advances.

We sincerely thank every reader who has accompanied us thus far. We hope the knowledge gained opens doors to creative applications, bold projects, and impactful solutions across various sectors of industry and research. May these pages serve as a recurring reference guide, a consultation resource, and a source of inspiration for solving complex problems, scaling cutting-edge models, and maintaining analytical quality throughout every stage of an AI project lifecycle.

On behalf of the entire team involved in the conception and

production of this book, we express our gratitude for the trust placed and the time invested in absorbing this knowledge. The deep learning universe is expanding rapidly, but the essence of machine learning—collecting, cleaning, analyzing, modeling, and deploying—remains anchored in sound software engineering principles, rigorous testing, version control, and collaboration.

We invite each reader to continue seeking new experiences and sharing results with the community, so that the cycle of innovation continues. There is always a new challenge awaiting intelligent solutions, and every technological domain is enriched when knowledge is shared and collectively built.

Move forward with the awareness that data science and deep learning are not ends in themselves, but tools in the service of real problems. Mastering Keras and knowing how to interact with essential libraries in the Python ecosystem, especially Scikit-Learn, enables professionals to transition from data exploration to the delivery of predictive services. The final message is one of encouragement: by uniting theory and practice, mastering pipelines and architectures, and applying solid software engineering principles, the bridge between idea and real-world solution becomes increasingly shorter and more productive.

Sincerely,
Diego Rodrigues & Team

www.ingramcontent.com/pod-product-compliance
Lightning Source LLC
La Vergne TN
LVHW051231050326
832903LV00028B/2348